FIFTY PLACES TO PADDLE

BEFORE YOU DIE

FIFTY PLACES TO

PADDLE

BEFORE YOU DIE

Kayaking and Rafting Experts Share
the World's Greatest Destinations

Chris Santella

FOREWORD BY ZACHARY COLLIER

STEWART, TABORI & CHANG

NEW YORK

This book is for my girls, Cassidy, Annabel, and Deidre.
I hope we'll have many fun days ahead on the water.

ALSO BY THE AUTHOR

The Hatch Is On!

Why I Fly Fish:
Passionate Anglers on the Pastime's Appeal and How It Has Shaped Their Lives

Fifty Places to Bike Before You Die:
Biking Experts Share the World's Greatest Destinations

Fifty Places to Fly Fish Before You Die:
Fly-Fishing Experts Share the World's Greatest Destinations

Fifty More Places to Fly Fish Before You Die:
Fly-Fishing Experts Share More of the World's Greatest Destinations

Fifty Places to Ski & Snowboard Before You Die:
Downhill Experts Share the World's Greatest Destinations

Fifty Favorite Fly-Fishing Tales:
Expert Fly Anglers Share Stories from the Sea and Stream

Fifty Places to Sail Before You Die:
Sailing Experts Share the World's Greatest Destinations

Fifty Places to Go Birding Before You Die:
Birding Experts Share the World's Greatest Destinations

Fifty Places to Dive Before You Die:
Diving Experts Share the World's Greatest Destinations

Fifty Places to Hike Before You Die:
Outdoor Experts Share the World's Greatest Destinations

Fifty Places to Play Golf Before You Die:
Golf Experts Share the World's Greatest Destinations

Fifty More Places to Play Golf Before You Die:
Golf Experts Share the World's Greatest Destinations

Once in a Lifetime Trips:
The World's Fifty Most Extraordinary and Memorable Travel Experiences

Contents

Acknowledgments 9 / Foreword 10 / Introduction 11

THE DESTINATIONS

(1) Alaska: Kenai Fjords 17
RECOMMENDED BY DAVID & WENDY DOUGHTY

(2) Antarctica: Antarctic Peninsula 21
RECOMMENDED BY AL BAKKER

(3) Arizona: Grand Canyon (Colorado River) 27
RECOMMENDED BY BRECK POULSON

(4) Australia: Tasmania (Southwest Coast) 31
RECOMMENDED BY MARK GRUNDY

(5) Belize: Ambergris Caye 35
RECOMMENDED BY LORI-ANN MURPHY

(6) Bhutan: Paro Chhu and Beyond 39
RECOMMENDED BY ZACHARY COLLIER

(7) British Columbia: Johnstone Strait 43
RECOMMENDED BY GRAHAM VAUGHAN

(8) British Columbia/Yukon/Alaska: Tatshenshini/Alsek Rivers 47
RECOMMENDED BY MELANIE SIEBERT

(9) California: Tuolumne River 51
RECOMMENDED BY NELSON MATHEWS

(10) Chile—Chiloé: Chiloé Archipelago 55
RECOMMENDED BY FRANCISCO VALLE GOMEZ

(11) Chile—Palena: Futaleufú River 59
RECOMMENDED BY ROBERT CURRIE

(12) Ecuador: Galápagos 65
RECOMMENDED BY MORAG PROSSER

(13) Fiji: Upper Navua River... 69
RECOMMENDED BY GEORGE WENDT

(14) Florida: Florida Keys 73
RECOMMENDED BY CAPTAIN BILL KEOGH

15 **Greece—Crete:** Crete (the South Coast) 76
RECOMMENDED BY KEITH HEGER

16 **Greece—Milos:** Milos 81
RECOMMENDED BY ROD FELDTMANN

17 **Hawaii:** Na Pali Coast 85
RECOMMENDED BY JOSH COMSTOCK

18 **Honduras:** Río Plátano 88
RECOMMENDED BY DR. CHRISTOPHER BEGLEY

19 **Iceland:** Hornstrandir (and Beyond) 93
RECOMMENDED BY RÚNAR KARLSSON

20 **Idaho:** Middle Fork of the Salmon 97
RECOMMENDED BY AL BUKOWSKY

21 **Idaho/Nevada/Oregon:** Owyhee River. 101
RECOMMENDED BY PETER GRUBB

22 **Indonesia:** Komodo Islands 105
RECOMMENDED BY PETER MILLER

23 **Italy:** Elba 109
RECOMMENDED BY BARBARA KOSSY

24 **Laos:** Mekong River 113
RECOMMENDED BY BRAD LUDDEN

25 **Maine—Bristol:** Greater Damariscotta River 117
RECOMMENDED BY TOM ARMSTRONG

26 **Maine—Princeton:** St. Croix River 121
RECOMMENDED BY ROB SCRIBNER

27 **Mexico—Campeche:** Campeche 125
RECOMMENDED BY MICHELLE BOWMAN

28 **Mexico—Loreto:** Sea of Cortez 128
RECOMMENDED BY NANCY MERTZ

29 **Minnesota:** Boundary Waters 133
RECOMMENDED BY BILL FORSBERG

30 **Montana:** Upper Middle Fork Flathead River 137
RECOMMENDED BY MIKE COONEY

31 **New Zealand:** Abel Tasman National Park 140
RECOMMENDED BY JACK KELLY

32 **Northwest Territories:** Nahanni River 145
RECOMMENDED BY NEIL HARTLING

33 **Ontario:** Cape Gargantua (Lake Superior) 149
RECOMMENDED BY JOANIE MCGUFFIN

34 **Ontario/Quebec:** Ottawa River 155
RECOMMENDED BY JIM COFFEY

35 **Oregon/Idaho:** Hells Canyon 158
RECOMMENDED BY PAUL ARENTSEN

36 **Oregon:** Rogue River 163
RECOMMENDED BY BRAD NIVA

37 **Panama:** San Blas Archipelago 167
RECOMMENDED BY JAVIER ROMERO GERBAUD

38 **Peru:** Tambopata River 170
RECOMMENDED BY KEN JOHNSON

39 **Quebec:** Magpie River 175
RECOMMENDED BY ERIC HERTZ

40 **Russia:** Kaa-Khem River 179
RECOMMENDED BY VLADIMIR GAVRILOV

41 **Scotland:** The Shetland Islands 183
RECOMMENDED BY ANGUS NICOL

42 **Texas:** Devils River 187
RECOMMENDED BY MARC McCORD

43 **Thailand:** Phang Nga Bay and Beyond 191
RECOMMENDED BY DAVID WILLIAMS

44 **Tonga:** Ha'apai & Vava'u 195
RECOMMENDED BY SHARON SPENCE

45 **United Kingdom:** South Georgia Island 199
RECOMMENDED BY RICK SWEITZER

46 **Vietnam:** Ha Long Bay 203
RECOMMENDED BY PATRICK MORRIS

47 **Washington—Cook:** Little White Salmon River 209
RECOMMENDED BY NICOLE MANSFIELD

48 **Washington—Friday Harbor:** San Juan Islands 213
RECOMMENDED BY TOM MURPHY

49 **West Virginia:** New and Gauley Rivers 217
RECOMMENDED BY RICK JOHNSON

50 **Zambia/Zimbabwe:** Zambezi River 221
RECOMMENDED BY JOHN BERRY

ACKNOWLEDGMENTS

This book would not have been possible without the generous assistance of the expert paddlers—kayakers, rafters, canoeists, and SUPers—who shared their time and experience to help bring these fifty great alpine venues to life. To these men and women, I offer the most heartfelt thanks. I also wish to acknowledge the fine efforts of my agent, Stephanie Kip Rostan; my editors, Samantha Weiner and David Blatty; the designer Anna Christian; and the copyeditor Suzanne Pettypiece, who helped bring the book into being. Finally, I want to extend a special thanks to my wife, Deidre, and my daughters, Cassidy and Annabel, who've humored my absence during seemingly endless deadlines . . . and to my parents, Tina and Andy Santella, who are not paddlers, but always encouraged me to pursue my passions.

OPPOSITE:
When paddling the marine-life-rich water around the Komodo islands, half of the attraction is below the surface.

FOREWORD

Paddling gets in your blood, flows to your core, and changes your life. Propelling yourself through water allows you to get intimate with a unique landscape, and every river trip has some impact on how you view your place in the world. From the peaceful solitude of kayaking a pristine creek or cove, to the special bonds you create with people you've shared an adventure with, each paddling experience solidifies the value of wild places.

Writing a list of "fifty places to paddle before you die" is a challenging undertaking. I've been a part of creating many "Top Ten Rivers of the World" lists that tend to get skewed by clever marketers with an agenda. It's hard to pick a mere ten locations when there are so many factors that converge to make a river trip truly incredible: accessibility, length of trip, difficulty, scenery, fishing, and wilderness character. Some of the places, like the Little White Salmon, are hair-raising and only accessible to the best paddlers in the world. Others, like the Grand Canyon, Middle Fork of the Salmon, or Rogue require experienced, but not expert, river runners. And there are also those great waters accessible by anyone with desire and a kayak, canoe, raft, stand-up paddleboard, inner tube, or inflatable whale.

I have had the privilege to paddle rivers all over the world, including nine of the rivers in this book. I can attest that every one of those nine is a world-class, bucket-list place to paddle. Chris Santella has interviewed some of the most knowledgeable paddlers on the planet to come up with the most comprehensive and accurate list of destinations I've ever seen. This book has reawakened my excitement and imagination for all of the paddling possibilities out there, and I look forward to paddling the forty-one places I have yet to experience.

—Zachary Collier, Northwest Rafting Company

INTRODUCTION

Starting from the very moment we're born, so many of us are drawn to water, be it rivers, oceans, or lakes. Propelling ourselves along by our own power adds an extra dimension to this time spent on the water.

I wrote *Fifty Places to Paddle Before You Die* for those who appreciate the exhilaration of running a rapid and the special sense of solitude that can be found paddling a secluded bay or river.

"What makes a destination a place you have to paddle before you die?" you might ask. "The chance to take in incredible mountain or coastal scenery? To push your skills to the limit on long endurance paddles or gnarly rapids? To encounter iconic animals that call the isolated places that can only be reached by raft or kayak home?" The answer would be yes to all of the above, and an abundance of other criteria as well. One thing I knew when I began this project: I was not the person to assemble this list. So I followed a recipe that served me well in my first ten Fifty Places books—to seek the advice of some professionals. To write *Fifty Places to Paddle Before You Die*, I interviewed a host of people closely connected with the paddling world—white-water rafters and kayakers, sea kayakers, SUPers, and canoeists—and asked them to share some of their favorite experiences. These experts range from competitive paddlers (like Zachary Collier and Nicole Mansfield) to travel specialists (like George Wendt and Peter Grubb) to adventurers (like Joanie McGuffin and Rick Sweitzer). Some spoke of venues that are near and dear to their hearts, places where they've built their professional reputations; others spoke of places they've only visited once, but that made a profound impression. People appreciate paddling for many different reasons, and this range of attractions is evidenced here. (To give a sense of the breadth of the interviewees' backgrounds, a bio of each individual is included after each essay.)

Paddling means different things to different people. For some, it may mean a three-hour excursion on bathtub-like calm/warm waters, with a late afternoon return to a shower and fine dinner; for others, it may mean running Class IVs in a northern wilderness, where the nearest shower may be the melt-off of a glacier. *Fifty Places to Paddle Before You Die* attempts to capture the spectrum of paddling experiences. While the book collects fifty great venues, it by no means attempts to rank the places discussed or the

quality of the experiences afforded there. Such ranking is, of course, largely subjective.

In the hope that a few readers are inspired to embark on their own adventures, I have provided brief "If You Go" information at the end of each chapter, including the level of difficulty of each experience (based on information provided by outfitters). This information is by no means a comprehensive list but should give would-be travelers a starting point for planning their trip. (As tastes and budgets may differ dramatically from individual to individual, I've tried to offer a general resource for lodging options. For some remote venues, only one option may be available, and it's been provided.)

Paddling can be a risky pastime, especially given some of the rapids that extremely advanced practitioners attempt to tackle. It should go without saying that kayakers, rafters, canoeists, and SUPers should always use good judgment and know their limitations.

One needn't travel to the ends of the earth to find a rewarding paddling experience. A calm day on a local river or bay can make for a great day. Yet a trip to a dream venue can create memories for a lifetime. It's my hope that this little book will inspire you to embark on some new paddling adventures of your own.

OPPOSITE:
The Rogue River in southern Oregon is one of the Northwest's quintessential rafting environments.

NEXT PAGE:
It's not hard to find a respite from the hustle and bustle of Phuket if you paddle out into Phang Nga Bay.

The Destinations

KENAI FJORDS

RECOMMENDED BY **David & Wendy Doughty**

"When people look up at the mountains that rise out of the sea here on the Kenai [Peninsula], they're a little thrown off," David Doughty began. "Sometimes they'll ask, 'What elevation are we at?' Thanks to the work of the fjords, we're blessed with an incredibly rugged and strikingly beautiful coastline, and that's certainly an important appeal to kayakers who visit. But that's just one aspect of the paddling experience. The waters here support big marine life—everyone has a picture in their mind of the breaching whales—but there's also smaller marine life that can be equally impressive, like a bay covered with millions of sea stars and jellyfish. People aren't expecting that. There's a very good chance you'll see black bears. And the experience of being near a glacier is both humbling and awe-inspiring. For me, it's the convergence of all these things that makes paddling the Kenai incredible."

It would be an understatement to say that Alaska has a great deal of shoreline to explore: 47,300 miles unfold from the northernmost reaches on the Beaufort Sea near Barrow to the southeast region that snakes along the northwestern edge of British Columbia. This staggering amount of terrain amounts to more shoreline than that of the lower forty-eight states combined! The relatively finite stretch from Seward to Sitka—a mere 500 miles from north to south, with just 15,000 miles of shoreline—sees the great majority of Alaska's recreational maritime traffic, much of this in the form of cruise ships plying the famed "Inside Passage." Cruise ship passengers get to take in some marvelous sites—Glacier Bay, for example—and have opportunities to purchase T-shirts and other assorted trinkets in each port of call. However, they miss the chance to tuck into more isolated fjords that small boat and kayak travel affords.

It's quite possible to conduct a do-it-yourself kayaking adventure around the Kenai; a shuttle boat can drop you near the section of coast you'd like to explore and retrieve you

OPPOSITE:
Aialik is one of
many glaciers
you'll encounter
in the Kenai.

at an appointed time and place. But given the region's propensity for wet, cool weather (it's classified as a rainforest, after all), the mothership option, where paddlers return to a boat to dry off and sleep each night, has its advantages. "Mothership trips give you great versatility in terms of covering lots of different areas—you can hit more highlights with the boat, especially if you have a finite period of time," Wendy Doughty added. "And there's something to be said for being able to come in from a paddle in the rain and have warm soup or tea waiting."

David and Wendy described some of the highlights of a six-day mothership trip that takes paddlers to Aialik Bay and Northwestern Lagoon. "We have a bit of a voyage to get to Aialik, but the boat follows the coastline, so it's really a wildlife safari," David continued. "We pass Spire Cove, where these immense rock formations jut out of the water, and we're almost sure to pass seals, sea lions, puffins, and a host of other sea birds, humpbacks, and—if we're lucky—orcas." "There's been a lot more humpback activity in the area in the last few years," Wendy said. "They've begun bubble net feeding, a behavior that we hadn't seen before around the Kenai. A few years back, we were going through Granite Passage (just west of Aialik Bay) in the boat, and there were eight humpbacks feeding in a channel. The captain pulled the boat into a protected area, and we dropped the kayaks in and paddled into the channel. The whales were circling us and feeding for several hours."

After reaching Aialik in the late afternoon, there's plenty of time for a paddle while dinner is prepared—perhaps in the shadow of a glacier or in an intimate cove. The following day, you may opt to explore Pedersen Lagoon, Abra Cove, or Aialik Glacier. "Pedersen Lagoon Wildlife Sanctuary is a wilderness area within Kenai Fjords National Park," David explained. "It can only be accessed by kayakers. The lagoon was created by the retreating Pedersen Glacier, which has a more sloping, gentle feeling than the other glaciers here. There's a tidal river at the end of the lower lagoon that gets significant runs of salmon, and the bear watching here can be great.

"Across the bay from Pedersen is Aialik Glacier. It's the classic [type of] glacier people expect to find in Alaska—1.2 miles wide and 300 to 500 feet high at its face. It's probably the most actively calving glacier in the park. If you're lucky, you can get front and center (a third mile back) and watch the falling ice. People are always surprised at how loud it is. There are usually large groups of seals—200 to 300—hauled out on the calved ice nearby. Abra Cove is nearby, and it's off the radar for many people. On a decent tide, you can paddle all the way to the back, along sheer rock walls that rise 1,500 feet in places. Abra holds snow year-round, and it's a novelty to paddle past a big wall of snow in August. This is a trip that's improved by the rain, as you'll get incredible waterfalls pouring down. We'll often see black bears swimming across the cove. When they land on shore, they shake like big dogs. It's just an hour paddle, but many visitors consider it the high point of the trip."

After a few days exploring Aialik Bay, you'll continue west toward Northwestern Glacier. En route, you'll likely visit Granite Island and paddle around Cataract Cove and Taz Basin. "Cataract Cove is U-shaped and very deep and has many waterfalls that you can kayak up to," David said. "Taz Basin is one of those places where sea stars and jellyfish are thick. It's a great place to cruise. Northwestern Glacier sits in the back of Northwestern Fjord. It's striking in that it's still very new. The glacier is moving back so quickly that it's pulling up the rock face at the edge of the fjord, even as it's calving ice. It's a very dynamic site, visually impressive, thanks to all the rock and ice; I've been watching it change from year to year. Because there's lots of ice, there are always lots of seals."

If time permits, David and Wendy may push farther west to Nuka Bay. "There's one main island at Nuka," Wendy said, "and a maze of hundreds of small, rocky outcroppings that you can paddle around. The appeal of Nuka for me is the isolation. There's lots of wildlife, including humpbacks. There aren't any glaciers there, but it has a subtle beauty of its own."

DAVID DOUGHTY is co-owner of Kayak Adventures Worldwide and Bear Paw Lodge. He has been leading trips—backpacking, canoeing, mountain biking, climbing, and kayaking—most of his life. He spent the first half of his working life as an acupuncturist and chiropractor and intends to spend the second half outdoors. David has an amazing enthusiasm for the sport of kayaking and even more for using the sport to share the area with others. He holds a current Wilderness First Responder certification, is a Leave No Trace trainer, an Alaska Tour Guide trainer, and a certified American Canoe Association sea kayaking instructor.

WENDY DOUGHTY is co-owner of Kayak Adventures Worldwide and Bear Paw Lodge. Originally from Connecticut, Wendy has spent many years traveling both within the States and internationally. She's enjoyed adventures that include reindeer herding near Antarctica, sailing the Mediterranean, living in the Swiss Alps, and working for *National*

Geographic. She holds a current Wilderness First Responder certification and is a Leave No Trace trainer. She's an American Canoe Association Level 4 certified paddler and Level 3 certified sea kayaking instructor, with endorsements to teach day trip leadership, kayak/camping, and rolling.

If You Go

▶ **Getting There:** Seward is the jumping-off point for the Kenai Fjords; it's roughly 120 miles south of Anchorage, which is served by many carriers.

▶ **Best Time to Visit:** May through August will provide the most temperate weather, but even then, temperatures will be cool, and you'll encounter periods of rain.

▶ **Guides/Outfitters:** There are a number of outfitters who lead trips around the Kenai. Kayak Adventures Worldwide (907-224-3960; www.kayakak.com) offers a host of multi-day trips, including mothership-supported trips.

▶ **Level of Difficulty:** Kayakers should have a moderate level of experience for paddling the Kenai.

▶ **Accommodations:** The Seward Chamber of Commerce Conference & Visitors Bureau (907-224-8051; www.sewardchamber.org) outlines lodging options for before and after your trip.

ANTARCTIC PENINSULA

RECOMMENDED BY **Al Bakker**

In an average year, the Antarctic Peninsula sees around twenty-five thousand tourists. Many people come on large cruise ships that must maintain a comfortable distance from terra firma. A lesser number of visitors travel on smaller vessels that can be maneuvered closer to the sixth continent's ice and rocks. And a still smaller number of travelers take to the icy waters in kayaks to experience the humbling power of Antarctica in a very intimate way.

"Every day holds wonders," Al Bakker began. "It might be close-up encounters with whales or paddling past colonies of penguins or seals sleeping on ice floes. Even though it's summer, the weather is uncertain. Some days will be 40°F with bright blue skies; other days it might snow or sleet. You have to go with an adventurous spirit because we never know exactly what awaits [us]. But this sense of surprise only enhances the sense that you're an explorer—which, in many ways, you are."

Antarctica is not one of the world's most welcoming places. There are no indigenous people on the continent, despite the fact that Antarctica encompasses over fourteen million square kilometers, roughly 1.5 times the size of the United States. (A contingent of five thousand scientists from the twenty-seven nations that are signatories of the Antarctic Treaty maintain a year-round presence on the continent. A great majority of the land mass—an estimated 98 percent—consists of ice and snow that has an average thickness of seven thousand feet; scientists believe that up to 70 percent of the world's fresh water is contained there. Put another way: If the ice stored in Antarctica were to melt, the world's oceans would rise 200 feet.) While precipitation can reach the equivalent of thirty-six inches of water on the Antarctic Peninsula, the continent's wettest region, only an inch of precipitation reaches the South Pole. During the winter

months, when temperatures hover in the range of -40°F to -90°F, seawater surrounding the continent freezes up to two hundred miles offshore, covering an area even larger than Antarctica's landmass. In the summer (December through March), temperatures rise to 32°F (or more), and a brief window opens for sailing to the more northerly portions of Antarctica. The continent is quite mountainous, with peaks (like Vinson Massif) over sixteen thousand feet; the lure of scaling a never-before-climbed peak has attracted many adventurers.

Suffice it to say, a kayaking trip to Antarctica is not well suited for the occasional traveler. First, there's the two-day crossing of the Drake Passage—almost five hundred miles, from Cape Horn to the Shetland Islands, at the northern tip of the continent. Even on an expedition cruise ship, there's a sense of exploration as you pass through "the roaring forties, the furious fifties, and the screaming sixties"—the unobstructed winds that howl through the passage, where waves can reach heights of sixty-five feet. As you push farther south, you'll pass through alleys of icebergs—cracking, rolling, with massive chunks calving off. Once you reach the calmer water of Bransfield and Gerlache Straits, you'll begin to disembark and paddle. "Most operators will do one or two outings a day," Al continued, "though of course, it always depends on the weather. I always recommend that visitors allot at least twelve days for a trip. This gives us six days around the peninsula, and you're almost certain to get some good weather. We provide dry suits with neoprene booties for paddlers, the same sort of outfit you'd use on a cold river. Generally, we'll go for a paddle after breakfast, return to the boat for lunch, and then have another paddle in the afternoon. If guests are more interested in spending time onshore, they can leave their kayak on board and take the Zodiac in."

The specific paddles required on each trip vary depending on conditions. A few places you might visit include Livingston Island, breeding ground for countless chinstrap and gentoo penguins, as well as giant petrels. Elephant seals—which can grow to be sixteen feet in length and weigh eight thousand pounds—are sometimes present as well. On Half Moon Island, there's a significant chinstrap penguin rookery, and fur and elephant seals are often hauled out on the pebble beaches. (One note: All of those National Geographic specials do not prepare you for the *scent* of a penguin colony.) Al shared a few of his favorite spots. "Lemaire Channel is always a highlight—if the ice allows us to go through. The cliffs tower almost 2,500 feet above the water, and there are incredible iceberg galleries. The water can be so calm, the cliffs are perfectly

OPPOSITE:
Paddlers near
Enterprise Island
enjoy a clear
day as they
return to the
Polar Pioneer.

reflected in it. Hydrurga Rocks is another highlight. These granite rocks are barely above the sea, but they are covered in wildlife—including Weddell seals and chin-straps—and the island is small enough to paddle around. *Hydrurga* is Latin for leopard seal, and we sometimes see these predators in these waters. [Leopard seals are the only seal that will devour other seals. They're easily identified by their slightly reptilian head and a white throat that's decorated with black spots.] They are curious, intelligent creatures and unpredictable. I've had them come over and investigate a group of kayaks, depart, and then return with a penguin, which they drop by the boats. I have no idea what this behavior means."

Al has made many trips to Antarctica and accumulated many memories. "I recall get-ting into my kayak in the late afternoon on one occasion, and a soft snow was drifting down. It was sticking to the surface a bit, and it felt as though I was paddling in a light porridge. A humpback whale surfaced just fifty feet away. Despite its great size, it was so quiet.

"Another time, a group of us had pulled out on some sea ice—which is quite stable—and we were enjoying a cup of tea. It was in the evening, and the sun was near the hori-zon, as close as you get to a sunset in the austral summer. Leopard seals will call to each other when they're out on the ice, and it's a very eerie sound. It was calm and quiet that evening, and we could hear these calls going back and forth, with the red sky in the back-ground."

AL BAKKER has paddled white water and sea kayaks for forty years in North America, South America, the South Pacific, Japan, Australia, New Zealand, Antarctica, South Georgia, the High Arctic and Greenland, the Russian Far East, and all across Europe. He has led commercial sea kayak tours for the last twenty-four years and developed sea kayak, rafting, and cross-country ski programs in many countries. Al has organized and led sea kayaking adventures in the polar regions for the past fourteen years. He is a qualified sea kayak instructor, Nordic ski instructor and examiner, swim instructor and examiner, and he holds swiftwater rescue and national lifeguard certification. Al has worked as a helicopter ski guide, rafting guide, and wilderness first-aid instructor and is a keen photographer. He has managed his own kayak tour company—Southern Sea Ventures—for more than two decades.

If You Go

▶ **Getting There:** Many ships heading for the Antarctic Peninsula depart from Ushuaia, Argentina. Service is available via Buenos Aires on Aerolíneas Argentinas (800-333-0276; www.aerolineas.com.ar) and LAN (866-435-9526; www.lan.com).

▶ **Best Time to Visit:** Expeditions are launched during the austral summer—November through March.

▶ **Guides/Outfitters:** Southern Sea Ventures (+61 2 8901 3287; www.southernsea ventures.com) offers kayak-oriented adventures to the Antarctic Peninsula.

▶ **Level of Difficulty:** Kayakers should have a moderate skill level . . . and be mentally prepared for very cold water.

▶ **Accommodations:** You can learn more about lodging options in Ushuaia for before and after your trip at www.tierradelfuego.org.ar.

GRAND CANYON (COLORADO RIVER)

RECOMMENDED BY **Breck Poulson**

"When people first call to inquire about rafting the Grand Canyon," Breck Poulson observed, "they ask about the rapids—how big are they, how gnarly. The night before the trip begins, it's still about the rapids. But when they've actually been out on the river for a few days, it's no longer about the rapids. It's about a life-changing experience, getting away from the real world, experiencing a genuine adventure and the magnitude of the canyon. By the end of the trip, the rapids are an afterthought."

Neither the deepest nor widest gorge in the world, the Grand Canyon is nonetheless recognized as one of the planet's most awe-inspiring erosion events—a 277-mile-long chasm that yawns from four to eighteen miles and reaches depths of more than a mile. Scientists believe human presence in the canyon dates back thirteen thousand years. It was not until 1869 that the first men of European descent, under the command of Major John Wesley Powell, navigated the Colorado's roiling waters. Powell (who had lost most of his right arm in the Civil War) and his nine fellow sojourners did not have the benefit of rubber rafts or detailed guide books; they ran the Colorado in wooden dories that had been built in Chicago and transported west.

The section of the Colorado River flowing through the Grand Canyon—either 186 or 225 miles, depending on where you take out—is one of the world's preeminent river adventures. Yes, there over forty rapids rated V or higher. Yes, the conventional rating scale of I to VI that's used on most western rivers is discarded in lieu of a 1 to 10 scale (with both Crystal and Lava Falls coming in at a solid "10"). But as Breck described, it's the hikes to hidden waterfalls, crystalline creeks, ancient Indian ruins, and the sandy campsites beneath unblemished night skies that make the Grand Canyon a must-float for any serious paddler. Though a finite number of permits for very experienced do-it-yourselfers

OPPOSITE:
Many rafters
come to the
Grand Canyon
for the rapids,
but they leave
enthralled with
its splendor
and side hikes.

are issued each year, most Grand Canyon rafters will opt to go with an outfitter. Oar boat trips take twelve, fourteen, or sixteen days. Breck, a veteran of more than one hundred Grand Canyon floats, described the dynamics of this epic adventure.

"On the night before the trip, when we do an orientation, people always have a deer-in-the-headlights look," he observed. "People are wondering what they've gotten into. After the put-in at Lee's Ferry, people are still wondering what they've gotten into. After the first few rapids, people are starting to get a feel for the canyon, but they're still in their own little groups. After the first night, people are discussing the night before, the moon, the stars. By the time we make our first stop and take our first hike, the different groups are starting to intermingle and form friendships. After running a few of the bigger rapids in the Inner Gorge (Unkar, Nevills, Hance, Sockdolager, and Grapevine among them), we're jelling together as a big river family working our way downstream."

The vistas of the canyon from the Colorado River are beyond words; in some places, rafts are more than a mile below the rim, which can't even be viewed from the water. As most days entail between three and five hours of floating, there's plenty of time to get out and explore the canyon. Breck described a few of his favorite hikes. "The first is at Nankoweap [Trail], where we can walk up to see the Ancestral Puebloan granaries. The Ancient Ones used crevasses in the rock to store grain and supplies after spending the winter months in the canyon. From the granaries, you can see all the way down to the canyon that forms the Little Colorado. It's an astonishing view, one of the best of the trip, and the hike only takes an hour. At mile 136, we reach Deer Creek Falls. You can hike above the falls to a point high above the Colorado. There's a spot here called 'The Patio' where Deer Creek gathers before heading for the falls. There's nice shade, and you can cool your feet off in the river. If you don't feel like hiking, you can swim in the pool that's created by the falls. The water's always clear."

Of the seventy-two named rapids that punctuate the Colorado's Grand Canyon stretch, Lava Falls—near the trip's conclusion—garners much of the mindshare. "People are talking about it all the way down," Breck added. "'What's it like? What's it like?' Anticipation certainly builds, to the point where people start picking out where they're going to sit in the boat when Lava is run. It's almost like a sporting event. When you get through, your team has won." In terms of overall difficulty, Breck places Hance, Horn Creek, and Crystal at the top of the list. In terms of overall fun, he likes Hermit. "Hermit always has five big roller-coaster waves," he continued. "Even our thirty-seven foot motor rafts can be buried in there. There are no big turns, no technical moves you need in Hermit. You just head down the middle of it and get soaked."

There have been many rapids for Breck Poulson to recollect from his many years on the Colorado, yet one of his fondest memories concerns a family he guided. "We had a father on one trip with two teenage daughters," he recalled. "It soon became apparent that the girls didn't want to go.

"On that same trip, we had an older man, close to eighty. It was obvious he was going to need some help, especially with the hiking. The crew managed to get the kids working together with the older guest, to the point where they were helping him on the hikes. As they began helping the older man, they started getting along better and better with their dad. It was fun to watch their change of heart and the evolution of their relationships with the older guest and their father."

BRECK POULSON took his first river trip through the Grand Canyon in 1973. Since then, he's been down the river more than one hundred times. Today, he serves as general manager of Wilderness River Adventures and director of tour operations at Lake Powell Resorts and Marinas.

If You Go

▶ **Getting There:** Groups generally assemble in Flagstaff, Arizona, which is served by several carriers, including Alaska Airlines (800-252-7522; www.alaskaair.com) and US Airways (800-428-4322; www.usairways.com).

▶ **Best Time to Visit:** Most commercial trips run between May and October.

▶ **Level of Difficulty:** Extreme for do-it-yourselfers. Inexperienced paddlers will be fine on guided trips.

▶ **Guides/Outfitters:** There are a number of outfitters authorized to lead trips through the Grand Canyon, including Wilderness River Adventures (928-645-6049; www .riveradventures.com).

▶ **Accommodations:** The Flagstaff Convention & Visitors Bureau (800-842-7293; www .flagstaffarizona.org) highlights lodging options for before and after your float.

TASMANIA (SOUTHWEST COAST)

RECOMMENDED BY **Mark Grundy**

"The southwest coast of Tasmania is a true wilderness," Mark Grundy began. "There are no roads, no settlements, and very few hiking tracks. It can be a harsh environment. Heavy trade winds—the roaring forties—blow through, bringing many heavy storms in the winter. This has discouraged modern human development. However, the winds begin to dissipate in late October, and by December, the waters here calm down and can be navigated by kayak. The landscape is dramatic in a stark sense. There are fantastic quartzite schist formations; in [some] places, 2,500-foot mountains drop straight into the ocean. In other places, the landscape allows long, unimpeded views—Tasmania's version of Big Sky country. Taking all this in by kayak allows you to really appreciate the grandeur. And if you're there in the early part of the season, you'd be hard pressed to see another person beyond those in your party."

The Australian state of Tasmania rests some 150 miles south across the Bass Strait from Melbourne; it's sometimes called "the island off the island." It's not the Australia people imagine based on tourism brochures of the mainland. For starters, it's considered the most mountainous island of its size in the world. Tasmania's Wilderness World Heritage Area covers nearly a fifth of the total area of the island, including Cradle Mountain–Lake St. Clair National Park, home of the famous Overland Track. The central island boasts some of the best-preserved temperate forests left in the world, not unlike what one might encounter in New Zealand or regions of South America. The coastline is stunning, with myriad coves, bays, beaches, estuaries, and spectacular cliffs. It's home to many of Australia's unique mammals, birds, and alpine plants.

There are three ways to reach Melaleuca, Mark's starting point for paddle explorations of the southwest Tasmanian coast: a five-day hike, a long boat ride, or a fifty-minute flight.

OPPOSITE:
Kayakers enjoy
a special sense
of isolation
in Bathurst
Harbour, off the
southwest coast
of Tasmania.

Mark opts for the flight. "The chance to fly over the Wilderness World Heritage Area is a unique facet of the adventure," he continued. "The pilot maneuvers through the rugged mountains or, if they're clouded out, along the coast. The swells are uninterrupted from Antarctica or South America, and the power is formidable. Before we begin exploring Bathurst Harbor and pushing out to more open waters, I like to hike up Mount Rugby. It's a steep hike to an elevation of over two thousand feet, but the reward is the best view in Tasmania, in my opinion. Bathurst Harbor is fed by several rivers, and where the tannin-stained freshwater meets with the salt water, there's a halocline. [With a halocline, the freshwater layers on top of the salt water. As a result, next to no light permeates the salt water, and this gives a variety of sea life—especially invertebrates—the impression that they are residing in water that's hundreds or thousands of feet in depth.] The western edge of the harbor is guarded by the Narrows, two peninsulas that squeeze in. Beyond the peninsulas are the Breaksea Islands, which form a natural breakwater for the harbor.

"Once you're out beyond the Breakseas, you're in Port Davey, which opens up to the Southern Ocean. Sometimes it's like glass; sometimes large swells are pounding the shore. We might cross Port Davey [it's really an inlet partially shielded from the open sea by Davey Head, not the American notion of a port] and head north up the Davey River gorge. Another option is to head south along the exposed coastline—true Southern Ocean paddling—on to Stephens Bay. Here, I like to visit the site of one of the largest Aboriginal middens on Tasmania. Many people don't realize that Tasmania was joined to Australia ten thousand years ago. As the ice receded and the sea levels rose, Tasmania was cut off. The Aboriginal people who lived on Tasmania were of the same lineage as those people on the mainland. Evidence suggests that humans have habituated Tasmania for thirty-five thousand years. This midden (or refuse area) still holds shellfish remnants that have been here for millennia."

Though the scenery is dramatic, you can't count on encountering Australia's totemic mammals along the coast in southwest Tasmania. "Thanks to the poor quality of the soil—due to the quartzite schist—the land just doesn't support that much fauna," Mark explained. "The flora is mostly button grass and low-lying melaleuca shrub, both very hardy plants. The same is true of the aquatic life, due to the infusion of freshwater in the area." While mammalian life is sparse, much of the region is considered an Important Bird Area, providing breeding ground for short-tailed shearwater, fairy prion, little penguin, and orange-bellied parrot, one of the world's rarest birds.

"One of the highlights for me of any southwest paddle is a trip to the Breaksea Islands off Port Davey," Mark said. "The western shore of the islands faces the ocean, and it can be fairly rough out there, but the eastern coast is usually quiet. By the time we reach the Breakseas, we've had four days together as a group. Normally, I try to get the group out there in the early evening, when it's still light enough to take in the huge landscape before us. Five minutes away, around the island, there's the fury of the roaring forties. But we're bobbing in a quiet, sheltered place, looking through the Narrows onto a mountain range. Sometimes it takes people thirty seconds, sometime five minutes, before it dawns on them that we're the only people there, the only people for many miles. No one else in the world is looking at what we're looking at. And we couldn't have gotten there without one another."

MARK GRUNDY and his wife, Jenny, operate Roaring 40s Kayaking and offer multiday sea kayaking adventures in the remote Tasmanian Wilderness World Heritage Area, day tours around Hobart exploring sea cliffs and watching for wildlife, and kayak instructional lessons. He is passionate about kayaking and the Tasmanian natural environment and loves sharing the area with guests.

If You Go

▶ **Getting There:** Trips begin and end in the Tasmanian capital of Hobart, which has regular service from Sydney and Melbourne via several carriers, including Virgin Australia (855-253-8021; www.virginaustralia.com/au) and Jetstar (866-397-8170; www .jetstar.com/au). A charter flight will take you to Melaleuca, where you'll begin paddling.

▶ **Best Time to Visit:** Winds and temperatures are mildest December through April.

▶ **Guides/Outfitters:** Roaring 40s Kayaking (+61 3 455 949 777; www.roaring40s kayaking.com.au) leads several different trips along the southwest coast of Tasmania.

▶ **Level of Difficulty:** Exceptional paddling skills aren't required, but visitors should be comfortable in a rugged outdoor environment.

▶ **Accommodations:** Discover Tasmania (www.discovertasmania.com) lists lodging options in Hobart.

AMBERGRIS CAYE

RECOMMENDED BY **Lori-Ann Murphy**

Belize is a small Central American country blessed with a very large reef. Formerly known as British Honduras, it's tucked on the southeastern quadrant of the Yucatán Peninsula, between the Quintana Roo province of Mexico to the north, Guatemala and Honduras to the west and south, and the western extremes of the Caribbean to the east. With much of its original rainforest intact, Belize has become a favored ecotourism destination in recent years for birders and those hoping to catch a glimpse of a jaguar, as the big cats still thrive here. Divers and snorkelers have long known Belize for the attractions of the Mesoamerican Barrier Reef, which stretches over four hundred miles along the entire Belizean coast, north to Quintana Roo, and south to parts of Guatemala and Honduras.

For many, the phrase Ambergris Caye is synonymous with Belize. The island—thirty-five miles northeast of Belize City—attracts the lion's share of international visitors, thanks to a mix of tourist infrastructure and easy access to the Mesoamerican Barrier Reef. Beyond the clear, sheltered Caribbean waters west of the reef, Ambergris has countless channels, lagoons, and mangrove marshes that are best explored by kayak. For Lori-Ann Murphy, kayaking around Ambergris means one thing: fishing. (Ambergris, incidentally, takes its name from the intestinal secretions of sperm whales, which the giant mammals occasionally vomit.)

"A kayak gives the angler or explorer access to the inner lagoons that big boats can't reach," Lori-Ann enthused. "The lagoons of Ambergris provide a safe nursery for the big three of saltwater flats fly fishing—bonefish, permit, and tarpon. The angler can get out of the boat and wade onto fish that are feeding way up in the lagoon on a high tide. For the explorer, kayaking offers up-close and personal exposure to some of Belize's beautiful birds, including roseate spoonbill or even a great horned owl."

OPPOSITE:
The crystal-line waters off Ambergris are a snorkeling and diving paradise—as well as a paddling paradise.

Much of the paddling on Ambergris is of the do-it-yourself nature, though lodges like El Pescador can provide good maps highlighting fishing hot spots, good birding locales, and secluded picnic/swimming spots. If you're especially ambitious, you can set out to tackle the route established for the Ambergris Caye Belize Lagoon Reef Eco-Challenge, a sixty-mile race that happens each June. The event was created by Ambergris business-man and environmentalist Elito Arceo to build awareness among his fellow islanders about the beauty of the lagoons on the backside of the island—lagoons that sometimes received less notice but were facing increasing development pressure. The circuit winds north from the town of San Pedro through a maze of lagoons and mangrove channels, finishing the first leg at the Bacalar Chico National Park and Marine Reserve, where the Mesoamerican Reef joins the mainland and Belize borders Mexico. (The park and reserve protect forty-one square miles of habitat that is home to jaguars and nesting loggerhead and green sea turtles.) The next day paddlers head south along the reef. "Professional kayakers come from all over the world to compete," Lori-Ann continued, "though pad-dlers of all levels are welcome to participate."

"The Bacalar Chico Reserve is going to be a great kayaking destination," Lori-Ann added. "It was once the site of a Mayan settlement; in fact, the Mayans built the channel that now separates Mexico and Belize. [Ambergris is actually not an island at all but an extension of the Yucatán.] There are several ruin sites that still have yet to be explored. The reserve is currently being developed by the Belize Fisheries Department. Part of the plan is to establish a camping/kayaking concession in the park."

The fish that call the flats and reefs around Ambergris Caye home attract anglers and snorkelers from far and wide. And on rare occasions, those anglers and snorkelers attract attention from another of the island's denizens—saltwater crocodiles. Though American saltwater crocodiles are the largest member of the crocodile family (averaging twelve feet in length, with specimens reaching over twenty feet), they are not as menacing as their Nile and Australian cousins, which take hundreds of human lives each year. They are generally most active at night, feeding on small mammals, birds, fish, and crabs—though when they show up on a flat, wading anglers tend to take notice. "One day I was fishing with Wil Flack (who owns Tres Pescados, a fly shop in San Pedro) out on a flat we'd kay-aked to," Lori-Ann recalled. "Wil was on the opposite side of this small lagoon, and we were both sunk up to our knees in the mud. There were armies of bonefish coming toward us. Suddenly I saw a large dark shape coming across the flat—a fish? 'Wil, it's a tarpon!' I shouted. The dark shape took clearer form when its long tail moved from side to side. 'Lori-Ann, it's a croc!' Wil yelled. Indeed it was. Wil kept fishing, but I was paralyzed. The crocodile moved between us and stayed there for what seemed like a very long time, though I think it was only thirty seconds. Finally it swam away.

"At the end of the day, I said to Wil, 'Can we just talk about the fact that we were wading with a crocodile?' Incidentally, the bonefishing was stellar."

LORI-ANN MURPHY is a registered nurse by training, but in 1994, she decided to leave the health-care field to become a fly-fishing guide and launched Reel Women Fly Fishing Adventures, which leads angling adventures in Idaho, Montana, and beyond. In 2009 El Pescador, a resort in Belize, asked her to become its director of fishing, a role she thoroughly enjoys. Today, she splits her time between Belize and the western United States, living a life of fly-fishing. Learn more about Lori-Ann at reel-women.com/rwblog.

If You Go

▶ **Getting There:** Ambergris Caye is reached via Belize City, which is served by several carriers, including American Airlines (800-433-7300; www.aa.com) and US Airways (800-428-4322; www.usairways.com). From Belize City, it's a twenty-minute flight to San Pedro via Tropic Air (800-422-3435; www.tropicair.com).

▶ **Best Time to Visit:** Conditions are conducive to kayaking (and fishing) throughout the year, though there's a bit more rain in the summer and always the chance of hurricanes in the early fall.

▶ **Guides/Outfitters:** Lori-Ann Murphy (reel-women.com) can help steer kayak anglers in the right direction.

▶ **Level of Difficulty:** Less experienced kayakers exploring the mangroves may need a map; those kayaking to the reef should have moderate experience.

▶ **Accommodations:** El Pescador (800-242-2017; www.elpescador.com) hosts anglers and ecotourists and can help kayak anglers find their way. Most of the other hotels on Ambergris Caye have kayaks available.

PARO CHHU AND BEYOND

RECOMMENDED BY **Zachary Collier**

"I was attracted to Bhutan," Zachary Collier began, "because, in many ways, I believe it's the last pure Buddhist country. The beliefs and mores of Buddhism are engraved in everyone's lives [there]. It's not just a religion but also a way of life. People in the West may imagine Tibet to be this way, but what they may be picturing is more alive and thriving in Bhutan. When I first visited [the country], I realized that it is defined by a series of river valleys. You start in one valley, go up over a tremendous pass, then down to another river valley, climb another pass, drop into another valley, and so on. Each valley used to be considered a separate kingdom, and each has its own feel."

Most westerners know little about Bhutan (the Land of the Thunder Dragon), a tiny country the size of West Virginia that's sandwiched between India to the south and Tibet and China to the north. That's largely because until 1974, tourists were not permitted to visit Bhutan. Today, a limited number of visitors are allowed, each paying a tariff of $200/ $250 a day. For their tariff, visitors get a visa, basic lodging, meals, and transportation. Visitors must also retain a certified guide for the entirety of their travels. Those fortunate enough to make the long journey are not disappointed. The Bhutanese are warm people, still very influenced by Buddhist traditions that seem mystical to the eyes of outsiders. Many people live closely with their animals, and each spring they herd their yak high up into the mountains to spend the summer grazing on alpine pastures. Fortified monasteries guarding ancient temples *(dzongs)* cling to hillsides, defying gravity, while the towering mountains reach high into the clouds. Perhaps this proximity to the heavens helps lend Bhutan its sacred aura.

With mountains reaching over twenty-four thousand feet, Bhutan has some drainages that offer hair-raising white water, as you can imagine. Zachary has opted to create

OPPOSITE:
A raft passes
beneath the
bridge at Dumtse
Lhakhang on
the Paro Chhu.

39

a different sort of trip. "I try to expose visitors to the culture and beauty of the country," he continued, "with rafting on some easier rivers mixed in to show Bhutan in a way that few other people have seen it. We'll sometimes see other tourists as we're floating. The way they look at us, it feels like we're part of the scenery, part of Bhutan."

The itinerary Zachary has assembled includes day floats on four clear-flowing rivers: Paro Chhu, Mo Chhu, Pho Chhu, and Thimphu Chhu. Zachary's favorite float may be on the Pho Chhu (Father river), as it affords the opportunity to drift up on Punakha Dzong. "Of the many dzongs I've visited, Punakha is one of the most impressive. It dates back to the 1600s and has survived six fires, two floods, and one massive earthquake, as well as attacks from the Tibetans. There were no nails used in its construction; it's all tongue and groove. It's not only a religious center, but it's also the center of government for the Punakha Valley. Anywhere else it might be a museum, but here it's part of everyday life. It's one thing to drive up to the renowned dzong in a tour bus. It's another to float past this humongous structure on a tiny raft. You can better appreciate the scope."

One of the high points off the water is a visit to Taktshang Goemba (Tiger's Nest), a three-hundred-year-old monastery perched precariously on a three-thousand-foot-high cliff above Paro Valley. It's a more than two-hour hike to reach Tiger's Nest. Its mirage-like visage slowly comes into focus as you near, and most feel the effort is well merited. Inside, giant clay buddhas painted a shimmering gold and murals of buddhas entwined with their consorts in tantric embraces await, and the altar is flush with plastic flowers, tarnished coins, butter sculptures, and food offerings.

"On my first trip, we happened to visit on a high holy day," Zachary recalled. "I was able to witness an amazing procession. There were monks chanting and blowing horns, with one senior monk presiding. At one point his cell phone rang, and he picked it up. For me, this moment captured Bhutan; it's a place that embraces the world, yet at the same time strives to keep its culture intact."

Some of life's best experiences occur spontaneously. In Zachary's experience, this is especially true in Bhutan. "On one trip, my group was hiking up to the put-in for our Pho Chhu float. We passed a family that was having their house blessed by a group of monks, and the family invited us to join them. They shared their food and the homemade wine they had for the occasion. Their generosity was tremendous. We put in on the river and began floating down. Pretty soon we came upon the monks who had blessed the house. They were playing this rock-throwing game (somewhat like bocce) down by the river. We weren't sure what to do—whether it was okay to stop and talk to them. They beckoned to us, and we stopped. Soon we joined them in the game. Though we couldn't communicate through speech, they gestured that they wanted to get in the raft. We got twelve monks into the raft and floated them downriver one hundred feet or so. I'm pretty sure they'd never been in a raft, and they were thrilled.

"And so were we."

ZACHARY COLLIER began his river career as a humble guide, and during the past fifteen years, he's worked with ten different outfitters on over thirty rivers in the United States, Costa Rica, Honduras, Chile, Bhutan, Nepal, and Siberia. He now lives in Hood River, Oregon, where he manages the day-to-day operations of Northwest Rafting and is able to get on the river all year long. Zachary is a board member of the Oregon Guides and Packers Association and an active member of America Outdoors, the national association for outfitters. He is also the rafting blogger for Travel Oregon, Yeti Coolers, and Best Made Company. As a competitive oarsman, he's won in the cataraft division at the Upper Klamath River Festival, the Upper Wind River Festival, and the Upper Clackamas Whitewater Festival, where he's won the oar boat slalom for the past four years and the cataraft slalom for the past three years.

If You Go

▶ **Getting There:** Bhutan is not easy to get to; it requires nearly twenty-four hours of flying time from New York City (via London, Bangkok, and Calcutta). Once you reach Asia, Drukair (www.drukair.com.bt) provides service to Bhutan from Calcutta, New Delhi, and Bangkok.

▶ **Best Time to Visit:** Northwest Rafting leads trips to Bhutan in November.

▶ **Guides/Outfitters:** Several outfitters lead rafting-oriented trips in Bhutan, including Northwest Rafting Company (541-450-9855; www.nwrafting.com).

▶ **Level of Difficulty:** This is first and foremost a cultural trip, with lots of rafting mixed in. It's fine for novice paddlers.

JOHNSTONE STRAIT

RECOMMENDED BY **Graham Vaughan**

"Visitors come to Johnstone Strait to be among the orcas," Graham Vaughan began, "but they're also looking for a wilderness adventure. You can get this experience on Johnstone Strait. The remoteness and serenity of the place, not to mention the abundance of wild-life—salmon, sea lions, seals, bald eagles, dolphins, and minke whales—make it a truly amazing place. What makes it even better is that it's fairly easily accessible."

Johnstone Strait stretches approximately seventy miles along the northeast coast of Vancouver Island. The channel—in places less than two miles wide—separates Vancouver from a number of smaller islands and the mainland. Large sections of the strait are set aside as the Robson Bight Ecological Reserve to provide a sanctuary for killer whales. The strait's narrow dimensions help explain the presence of approximately 230 orcas—members of British Columbia's Northern Resident population. "All the islands in the narrow strait serve to constrict water flow," Graham explained. "When the tide rises and falls, there's a massive water movement. This brings up nutrients for smaller creatures to feed on, which in turn engages the entire food chain, all the way up to the orcas."

Male orcas can reach a length of twenty-seven feet and a weight of eight tons. They spend their entire life with the group (or pod) into which they were born; when an orca is born, the entire pod works together to raise it. Despite their fearsome nickname—"killer whales"—orcas have not been known to show aggression toward humans but do feed aggressively on salmon and seals. "Most of the orcas we see in the strait are resident ani-mals and feed primarily on any of the five salmon species on the coast . . . though they prefer Chinook for their fatty meat," Graham explained.

Graham described a typical day at Spirit of the West's Johnstone Strait camp. "Guests sleep in tents mounted on platforms. Everyone opens up their fly to a view of Johnstone

OPPOSITE:
Johnstone Strait
is one of the most
reliable spots in
the world where
you can paddle
with orcas.

Strait. After a hearty breakfast, we'll head out for a two- or three-hour paddle before lunch. We can't guarantee that you'll come upon pods of whales, as nature is nature and the whales are following the fish. But over the course of a four-day trip, we generally do. The experience of being among the whales is different for everyone. Some people are silent, as though they can't believe it's happening. Others are screaming. I've seen people cry or get so excited that I have to tell them to calm down so they don't capsize their kayak. We usually have a hydrophone in the water, so you can also listen to what's happening."

The site of Spirit of the West's camp, incidentally, is the spot where musicians would once assemble in the late 1960s with wind and string instruments to play as a means of communicating with the whales.

"After the morning paddle, we'll find a nice beach for lunch. One of my favorite spots is next to the Robson reserve. Another beach is below the killer whale research station. You can hike up the bluff and look out over the strait. After lunch, we'll paddle back toward camp. We have a wood-fired saltwater hot tub fifteen feet up from the water. Sometimes you can see whales swimming by. We take pride in our food at camp, and we try to step it up, even though we're in a remote location. One of the standout meals is our maple-glazed wild sockeye salmon, with fingerling potatoes, beet-carrot green salad, and freshly baked baguettes. We might top it off with a dessert of chocolate fondue. After dinner, there's a campfire, and we'll sometimes do an interpretive presentation on the wildlife of the region, First Nations history, or west coast forest ecosystems. In June and July, it's light until 11 P.M., so we're able to cram lots of activities in a day."

Even if no orcas are present, most paddlers who visit Johnstone Strait will leave with a heightened appreciation of the beauty of unspoiled coastal British Columbia. "On our six-day expedition trip, we bob and weave between the archipelago of islands— sometimes foggy, sometimes sunny—you can easily forget that there's a world outside," Graham added. "Both the six-day expedition and the four-day basecamp trips are very forgiving for inexperienced kayakers. Even if the wind picks up in the afternoon to ten to fifteen knots or more, you can always find shelter in the islands and pick an easier route back to camp."

Regulars at Johnstone Strait have had the chance to witness an array of interesting orca behaviors, including the animals coming up in the shallows to "beach rub" against the pebbled bottom. (It's unclear whether this is done to remove parasites or for the sheer tactile pleasure.) One of the most memorable orca spectacles that Graham has witnessed came in the summer of 2012. "We were near the shore and came upon a resting line of twenty-three orcas," he recalled. "When the whales are in a resting line, half of their brains are turned off, and they're sleeping. [Only] the animals on either end are [fully] awake and guiding the group along. The whales were all abreast, moving slowly. We watched them for half an hour. I think everyone in our group connected with the moment, with where they were and what was happening. That's one of those experiences where, many years after the trip, you picture yourself back in the moment."

GRAHAM VAUGHAN is a Level 3 sea kayak guide and guide trainer with the Sea Kayak Guides Alliance of BC and guides year-round with Spirit of the West Adventures based on Quadra Island. He is an outdoor enthusiast and lives for his time spent in the natural world. A Wilderness Leadership Program and Outdoor Recreation Management Graduate from Capilano University, Graham has a passion for educating and inspiring others. Abroad, he has guided kayaking in Patagonia and the Bahamas, done aid work in Paraguay, and guided white-water rafting and canoe trips in New Zealand and British Columbia since 2006. When he is not kayaking, Graham fills his days mountain biking and skiing around his home on Quadra Island.

If You Go

▶ **Getting There:** The Spirit of the West kayak camp is reached by boat via Campbell River, which is served by Air Canada (800-776-3000; www.aircanada.com) from Seattle and Vancouver.

▶ **Best Time to Visit:** Orcas are generally present from late June through late September. Your odds of killer whale encounters increase later in the season.

▶ **Guides/Outfitters:** Spirit of the West Adventures (800-307-3982; www.kayakingtours .com) has guided kayakers on the Johnstone Strait from a permanent camp based on the strait since 1996.

▶ **Level of Difficulty:** Paddling on this trip is beginner friendly.

▶ **Accommodations:** Campbell River Tourism (campbellrivertourism.com) lists a range of lodging options for on your way to and from the Johnstone Strait.

TATSHENSHINI/ALSEK RIVERS

RECOMMENDED BY **Melanie Siebert**

Vast glaciers. Immense spires. Untrammeled wilderness. A lake filled with icebergs. All this (and much more) awaits on the Tatshenshini, perhaps the most renowned of Alaska's many rugged, runnable rivers.

"The Tat is a river of immense proportions, both in terms of rock and water," began poet and guide Melanie Siebert. "It's intimate at the outset, then makes its way through massive coastal mountains hung with incredible glaciers, then this immense glacier-carved valley, and finally Alsek Lake. At the confluence with the Alsek, the river is three miles wide, a massive pulsing muscle of a river. You feel at times like the glaciers receded just yesterday—you get a sense of the geological powers at work, a cycle of destruction and rebirth. The contrast between the rugged mountains and the wildflowers in the valley is intoxicating."

The Tatshenshini begins its course to the Pacific in British Columbia and rolls north to the southwestern Yukon before returning to British Columbia and joining the Alsek, which reaches the Gulf of Alaska at Dry Bay. Most groups that run the Tat will begin on the Klukshu River near Dalton Post, Yukon. From here, it's 160 miles through the world's largest biological preserve to the take-out. Most groups will allot eight to ten days on the river to leave time for exploratory hikes and general wonderment. Melanie shared some of her favorite moments from the many times she's floated the Tat.

"The second day on the river brings you to the Tatshenshini Canyon, a beautiful stretch of Class III white water and fun, thrilling chutes. It's quite narrow, with lots of twists and turns and some nice must-make moves. It's an exciting start. Over the next few days, the river builds very quickly, like a symphony with the different instruments entering. While we're in the valley section of the float, there's a good day hike I love to do to a

OPPOSITE:
The epic
Tatshenshini
float has many
high points,
perhaps topped
by the chance
to skirt icebergs
in Alsek Lake.

spot called Sediment's Creek. There are some great views of the Alsek Range from here, and you'll often see mountain goats up in the crags. They're incredibly agile creatures."

Downstream, the river begins to braid up. Some of Alaska's totemic animals—including moose and grizzly bears—are often encountered (at a safe distance!) on the gravel banks; bald eagles are almost as common here as pigeons are in Manhattan. If you get clear weather, the peaks of the St. Elias Range—including Mount Logan (19,551 feet) and Mount St. Elias (18,008 feet)—come into view. As you approach the confluence with the Alsek, the river becomes surrounded by glaciers; at one point, twenty-seven different glaciers are in view. Melanie likes to make camp near Walker Glacier. "It's a massive waterfall of ice, pouring toward the river," she explained. "We camp on a terminal moraine. You can feel the cold draft coming down off the ice. You can hike along the lateral moraine and get out on the glacier itself. It's a chance to get close to this eerie, other-worldly ice, with incredible crevasses, water holes, and seracs. All the while, [the water is] slowly flowing beneath you.

"At the confluence with the Alsek, there are so many braids that it's like a vast network of different rivers. This is another great spot to see bears as they fish for salmon. Eagles are on hand to scavenge. You see the whole food chain in action. The guides have a game that we play during this section called Spawning. The river is moving fast and has a silty steel-gray color from the rock flower (or glacial till). It's hard to tell how deep it is, and it's easy to get pushed up on the gravel—that is, 'spawned.' If you spawn, you owe the other guides a case of beer when the trip is done. When we get close to Alsek Lake, we'll pull the rafts over and hike up a scree slope to suss out the channels going into the lake. You don't want to pick a channel that's clogged with icebergs.

"One of my favorite camping spots on the trip comes on Alsek Lake. We stay on an island, and there are glaciers circling the lake, including Alsek and Grand Plateau, which stretch several miles. The glaciers are constantly calving, sending huge slabs of ice into the lake. You're in this incredible presence of thundering glaciers. Thanks to the calving glaciers, the lake is full of massive icebergs. I like to spend two nights at the lake so we can have a day to row around and explore. To me, the icebergs seem like living beings, strange avant-garde sculptures. As they melt, the icebergs turn over, exposing a glossy blue underside. They can turn over quickly, so we keep a healthy distance. There are lots of smaller chunks of ice in the lake—we call them bergy bits. There are times the bergy bits are so thick, you feel like the camp can get locked in by ice. I have to say that the bergy bits are perfect for margaritas. You can release a burst of ten-thousand-year-old air into your drink." From Alsek Lake, it's a short float to the Pacific. Here, peaks like Mount Fairweather soar more than fifteen thousand feet into the air.

While Alsek Lake may be Melanie's favorite camp spot on the Tatshenshini expedition, one of her favorite memories hails from another campsite upstream. "We were staying at a place called Milt Creek, and I had set up my tent close to the edge of the creek's bank. The creek funnels off a glacier, and that night, the water was rising. As I was sleeping with my ear to the ground, I could hear the booming sound of the boulders rolling along the creek bottom. The sound was being transmitted through ground, the song of the shaping of the landscape via the water."

MELANIE SIEBERT grew up paddling Canadian Shield rivers. She has guided for Nahanni River Adventures since 2000. Her book, *Deepwater Vee*, which was a finalist for a Governor General's Literary Award, features a suite of river poems subtitled with the GPS coordinates of some of her most memorable spots on the rivers she loves—the Nahanni, the Tatshenshini/Alsek, the Burnside, and the Thelon. In the winter, she teaches creative writing at the University of Victoria and works as a volunteer counselor at Citizens' Counselling Centre. In the spring of 2013, she was the writer-in-residence at the Berton House Writers' Retreat in Dawson City, Yukon.

If You Go

▶ **Getting There:** Whitehorse, Yukon, is the beginning and ending point for most Tatshenshini trips. It's served by several carriers, including Alaska Airlines (800-252-7522; www.alaskaair.com) and Air Canada (888-247-2262; www.aircanada.com).

▶ **Best Time to Visit:** Trips are conducted from June through early September.

▶ **Guides/Outfitters:** There are a number of outfitters who lead trips on the Tatshenshini. Canadian River Expeditions (800-297-6927; www.nahanni.com) offers trips on the Alsek as well as the Tatshenshini.

▶ **Level of Difficulty:** For guided trips, the paddling is classified as beginner level.

▶ **Accommodations:** Canadian River Expeditions lists some recommended hotels in Whitehorse for the beginning and end of your trip at nahanni.com/planning-your-trip.

TUOLUMNE RIVER

RECOMMENDED BY **Nelson Mathews**

"I grew up in Placerville, a town in the foothills of the Sierra Nevada gold country," Nelson Mathews began. "The American River runs near town. My mom met a guy who ran river trips on the American and a few other rivers, and he was looking for local kids to guide. I started working on the American. There were fun white-water sections, but it was mostly about people kicking back and having water fights. I kept hearing the other guides talking about the Tuolumne in hushed tones. The following year, I began my training on the Tuolumne. It was quite a different animal, to say the least."

The Tuolumne holds an esteemed place among members of California's paddling community; it's a venue that combines unspoiled gold country scenery, classic campsites, and abundant Class IV+ white water with relative accessibility. The river begins in Yosemite National Park near its namesake Tuolumne Meadows and flows 156 miles, mostly west, to its confluence with the San Joaquin near Modesto. Though long inhabited by the Miwok Indians (the Tuolumne was named for one of the tribes that lived in the valley), the Tuolumne first came to the attention of Anglos when gold was discovered in the region in the late 1840s. (Though many recognize 1848 as the beginning of the California gold rush, gold had been discovered and reported in 1842, near present-day Los Angeles.) The Tuolumne was the unofficial southern boundary for Sierra Nevada prospectors, though by the mid-1850s most had left; remnants of their brief visitation can be spied in the canyon in the shape of old cabins and abandoned mine shafts. The river would be forever altered to slake the thirst of the San Francisco Bay Area's swelling population. In 1913, construction began on the O'Shaughnessy Dam, which backed up the Tuolumne to flood the Hetch Hetchy Valley, an expanse of land that many considered as spectacular as Yosemite Valley. Not even the passionate appeals of naturalist and Sierra

OPPOSITE:
Clavey Falls—
the showcase drop
on the Tuolmne.

DESTINATION 9

Club founder John Muir could dissuade the city of San Francisco and the U.S. Department of the Interior from its reclamation plans . . . though not all of the river was lost.

For rafters and kayakers, the section of the Tuolumne that holds the greatest interest is the eighteen miles that flow through the pine- and scrub-oak-peppered canyon from near the town of Groveland to just above the Don Pedro Reservoir. In this brief stretch, there are more than twenty Class IV rapids, plus one Class V—Clavey Falls. "You get the sense that you're in a very isolated, remote place, even though you're in California and within one hundred miles of millions of people," Nelson continued. "It's usually pretty hot in the summer, approaching 100°F. But the water is pleasantly cool. And you get a chance to cool down pretty quickly, as the Tuolumne starts out with a bang—there are two Class IVs within the first half mile of the put-in at Meral's Pool. There's lots of moving, dodging, taking drops, riding big waves." Like most snowmelt-fostered rivers, the Tuolumne experience varies greatly depending on the time of year you run it. Rapids that might offer playfully rolling waves in May are highly technical rock gardens come mid-July. Nelson shared a few of his favorite sections.

"Rock Garden is the first rapid, and it requires some technical moves to get you from river right to river left. Nemesis is next, and there's a slot you have to hit or else you have a good chance of wrapping your boat. Sunderland's Chute (named for Dick Sunderland, one of the first kayakers to run the Tuolumne) comes after Nemesis. One of the two times I flipped a boat was at Sunderland's; one second my paddle boat was hitting a wave, the next, I was watching one of my raft mates drift past me. A little ways down you come to Ram's Head. Here, the river takes a big, sweeping turn to the left, where a rock face creates a curling wave and a hole. When my brother, Walt, and I were training during high water to run the river with guests, one of the trainees was distracted by the gaping maw below and wrapped a raft on a rock just above the big hole. My brother and I went back with some senior guides to try to recover it. We got a line out to the raft, and Walt and I volunteered to go out hand over hand to the rock. We tried deflating the raft but couldn't get it off. Eventually, we started returning hand over hand, only to have the rope break free. Luckily it stayed tied to a tree, penduluming us both back to shore rather than the far less attractive alternative. We probably should have checked the rope."

Clavey Falls is the Tuolumne's signature rapid, a Class V that earns successful boatsmen and women serious bragging rights. It's formed where the Clavey River enters the Tuolumne. "Some people will do the Tuolumne over several days," Nelson explained, "and there are some great campsites just above Clavey Falls. If I was running a multiday trip, I'd always try to camp at one of these sites so you could hear the roar of the river as you went to sleep. It would certainly give you some butterflies. Right as the Clavey comes in, the river drops significantly, ten or twelve feet; this is the falls. The current pushes you against the cliff face, and there's a big hole you try to navigate around. That's the place where I had my second flip, in an eighteen-foot raft. We went nearly end over end! If you can thread the needle between the cliff face and the hole, you'll generally pop out cleanly." Doing the river over several days allows time for some hiking up the side canyons (like the Clavey River and the North Fork of the Tuolumne) and for trout fishing.

Not long after Nelson began being mentored on the Tuolumne, the river faced its second great threat—a hydroelectric project (again, championed by the city and county of San Francisco) that would place three dams in the eighty-three-mile section of river between Hetch Hetchy and the Don Pedro Reservoir, essentially eliminating the river's white-water attractions. "I remember seeing the helicopters flying in and out as they were surveying the river," Nelson recalled. "It was not long after the flooding of the Stanislaus River [not far north of the Tuolumne], where Mark Dubois had chained himself to a rock in protest. Mark and Friends of the River, the organization that formed to oppose the dam project, lost that battle. But a lot of people in the rafting community were mobilized. When the Tuolumne proposal came up, the Tuolumne River Trust was formed. The trust and other committed parties were able to defeat the dam proposal and gain 'Wild and Scenic' designation for the Tuolumne between the O'Shaughnessy Dam and Don Pedro.

"The successful fight to save the Tuolumne had a huge impact on me. It inspired me to go to law school . . . though rafting had ruined me for being wrapped up in a three-piece suit every day. I ended up as the Western Rivers program director for the Trust for Public Land, protecting and providing access to wild rivers."

NELSON MATHEWS began working as a river guide back in 1980 on the American River near his hometown of Placerville, California. He is currently the chairman of the board for ARTA River Trips. When not floating down rivers, Nelson is the West program director for the Trust for Public Land (TPL), where he works to conserve land both along rivers and elsewhere. During his twenty-two years at TPL, Nelson has successfully negotiated, acquired, and conveyed into protective public and nonprofit ownership well over one hundred thousand acres of land with recreational, historic, and environmental significance.

These accomplishments range from protecting more than fifty-four thousand acres of watershed on the St. Joe River in northern Idaho with working forest conservation easement to helping create a thirty-two-acre new urban state park from an old rail yard in downtown Los Angeles. Nelson; his wife, Joanne; daughter, Casey; and son, Theo, live along the Deschutes River in Bend, Oregon. Nelson earned a BA in economics from UC Davis and a law degree from UCLA. He is a member of the State Bar of California. He is also an avid fly fisherman and skier.

If You Go

▶ **Getting There:** Groveland, the staging area for Tuolumne trips, is roughly three hours from the Bay Area and Sacramento, which are served by many carriers.

▶ **Best Time to Visit:** Commercial trips are run from early April through early September. Flows are significantly higher in the early spring.

▶ **Guides/Outfitters:** A number of rafting companies lead one- and multiday trips on the Tuolumne, including ARTA River Trips (800-323-2782; www.arta.org).

▶ **Level of Difficulty:** On guided trips, less seasoned paddlers will be fine; self-guided paddlers should have extensive white-water experience.

▶ **Accommodations:** The Groveland Hotel (800-273-3314; www.groveland.com) and the Hotel Charlotte (209-962-6455; www.hotelcharlotte.com) are both in Groveland.

CHILOÉ ARCHIPELAGO

RECOMMENDED BY **Francisco Valle Gomez**

All rivers (most of them, anyway) ultimately lead to the sea. It was a river that led Francisco Valle Gomez to the Chiloé Archipelago, though not in the typical gravity-driven sense.

"I had been in the river-running business in Chile on the Bìo-Bìo River from 1984 to 1995," Francisco began. "When the river was dammed, I was fed up with the management of rivers in Chile and began to look for opportunities in the sea. If you look at a map, you'll see that from Puerto Montt on to southern Patagonia, there's a crazy patchwork of mountains, fjords, and islands. Looking at this, I realized that we had a comparative advantage in sea kayaking and shifted my energies to this endeavor, focusing on two destinations: Chiloé and, to the east, the Andean fjords of Pumalín Park. The fjords region is about big, dramatic nature. The mountains plunge into the sea from heights of five thousand feet; the virgin forests are lush. Overall it gives you the feeling of wilderness. The archipelago is another type of landscape altogether, green but softer, less mountainous, and more impacted by humans. The attraction of Chiloé is really its people. Though they're Chilean citizens, the Chiloé have their own culture, and kayaking is a great way to experience it."

The Chiloé Archipelago and Pumalín Park are both in the Los Lagos region, in the northern reaches of Chilean Patagonia. Pumalín Park is on the mainland and is home to a pristine temperate rainforest of broad-leaved evergreens, among thousands of other plants. There are a number of islands that make up the archipelago, with Chiloé being by far the largest and home of the archipelago's two largest towns, Castro and San Juan. Francisco likes to begin paddling tours of the region with a few days around Pumalín. Here, you'll have the chance to paddle Quintupeu, Cahuelmo, and Comau Fjords. "All the fjords are extremely impressive," Francisco continued. "The entrance to Quintupeu is

55

very narrow, not more than one hundred meters wide. When you pass through, it opens up to views of snowcapped mountains; lush, hanging forests; and waterfalls. If it's a clear day, there's an incredibly blue sky above, though even on misty days, it's spectacular. There are often dolphins in the fjord, and they like the company of our kayaks.

"After exploring Quintupeu and a night camping in the fjord, we return to our mothership and head on to Cahuelmo Fjord. The weather can change very fast in the fjord region, and being able to get out of the elements on the support ship—and take our meals—is a nice luxury. There are often sea lions at the entrance of Cahuelmo. We can get close enough to see them quite well; you can smell them from a great distance! A real treat awaits at the far end of the fjord: Cahuelmo Hot Springs. Here, and again at Porcelana Hot Springs in Comau Fjord, you can enjoy a natural hot bath. The views of snowcapped peaks in Comau are especially stunning as you paddle to the back of the fjord, which showcases waterfalls among the unspoiled forests."

After a few days of exploring the fjords, Francisco likes to head west across the Chacao Channel to the island of Chiloé. Originally inhabited by the nomadic Chonos people, who made their living by fishing, and later the Huilliche, who both fished and farmed, Chiloé was discovered by Spanish sailors in the mid-1500s and was soon colonized. The cultures mixed to create the distinctive Chilote personality and way of life, not quite Chilean, not quite Spanish, with hints of the old Indian practices. (Chiloé, incidentally, was one of the last strongholds of Spanish rule in Chile, resisting home rule for several years after Chilean independence.) "In many of the villages on the archipelago, people are living as they've been living for hundreds of years," Francisco said. "Little has changed."

Two facets of Chiloé that are emblematic of the region are its stilt houses and its churches. The stilt houses—or *palafitos*—speak to the close connection Chilotes have with the sea. "One village I like to visit is Mechuque, which is on the little archipelago of Chauques, on the eastern side of Chiloé Island," Francisco continued. "Mechuque is made up mostly of stilt houses. Half of the house is over the water, and there are two fronts, one facing the street, the other, the sea. At high tide, the water is nearly up to the front door, and we can paddle among the houses. Residents can bring their boats almost to their door. At low tide, people can gather razor clams, mussels, and other shellfish from below the houses, which are constructed of distinctive shingles." The shellfish that are harvested are layered with pork, chicken, and potatoes and cooked on hot stones to create *curanto*, one of Chiloé's traditional dishes.

OPPOSITE:
Thick forests,
glaciers, and
snowcapped
mountaintops
come together in
Pumalin Park,
east of Chiloe.

Chiloé's churches, a testament to the Spaniard's missionary zeal, dot the islands of the archipelago. More than sixty were constructed in the eighteenth and nineteenth centuries and are considered unique for their wooden architecture—local larch, coihue, and cypress—which are weathered due to climate. Sixteen of the churches have been declared UNESCO World Heritage sites. "For me, one of the most striking examples of the wooden churches is the church of San Juan in the village of San Juan," Francisco added. "San Juan is also known for its two-hundred-year tradition of wooden boat building. When we visit, we usually see men working on boats, which are brightly painted when they're completed. I should add that since almost all the villages were built on the water, many of the old churches can be viewed from your kayak. It's a special vantage point."

FRANCISCO VALLE GOMEZ is a native Chilean and studied tourism enterprises at the University of Madrid, Spain. Founder of Altue, Chile's pioneer adventure travel company, he introduced white-water rafting to his compatriots for the first time. Since 1978, he has investigated the geography, history, and culture of his country, constantly exploring new places for sea kayaking and making first descents of rivers that are now considered famous adventure destinations. He has a passion for nature and a deep understanding of traditional cultures that he loves to share with his travel companions. During the summer, Francisco is usually found in Chiloé Island (Northern Patagonia) operating sea kayaking trips in the Andean fjords and archipelagic Chiloé.

If You Go

▶ **Getting There:** Trips begin and end in Puerto Montt, which is served by LAN (866-435-9526; www.lan.com) via Santiago.

▶ **Best Time to Visit:** The austral summer: December through March.

▶ **Level of Difficulty:** Beginners will have no difficulty with this trip.

▶ **Guides/Outfitters:** Several companies lead trips in the greater Chiloé region, including Altue Sea Kayaking (+56 09 4196809; www.seakayakchile.com).

▶ **Accommodations:** Visit Chile (www.visitchile.com) lists lodging options in Puerto Montt.

FUTALEUFÚ RIVER

RECOMMENDED BY **Robert Currie**

If you were to ask a roomful of rafting aficionados to name the greatest stretch of white water in the world, there would be lively debate. The Zambezi below Victoria Falls might make the shortlist. Perhaps the last day on a typical Grand Canyon float, too. But you can be almost sure that a good many would place Chile's Futaleufú at the top of the list.

"Some people consider the Futaleufú the Everest of rivers," Robert Currie began. "Back in the eighties, it had the reputation of being pretty much unrunnable. When my friend and business partner Eric Hertz checked it out, he thought it could be done as a commercial trip. But early efforts with conventional gear boats—metal frame, aluminum dry boxes, center mounts—didn't work. The river required too many moves, and the gear boats were too heavy. He thought it could be approached with a different kind of raft—an eighteen footer with a stern frame and paddles in front. This made it lighter and more maneuverable. With this setup, it could be done." And Robert and Eric were part of the team that made the first raft descent in 1991.

The Futaleufú begins on the Argentine side of the Andes in northern Patagonia and roars one hundred miles through Chile before entering the Pacific. Its appeals are many: its trademark turquoise blue waters, the result of its glacial origins and white granite bottom, which reflects the light; its incredible scenery, marked by soaring granite walls that are topped by primeval forests of pine and hardwoods with glacier-ringed mountains farther in the distance; and of course, its thirty-six Class IV and Class V rapids. Few if any other rivers combine the Futaleufú's beauty and its supercharged white water. (The upper forty miles of the river hold the lion's share of its famed rapids.)

The experience of running the "Fu" has evolved significantly from the early days. "We realized that even with the modified boat design, the river was too challenging for extended

DESTINATION 11

trips with baggage boats," Robert recalled. "First, we established a base camp and would access different stretches of the river from a dirt road. You'd run a section, return to camp, drive farther upstream the next day and run another section, then return to camp. It meant a lot of driving. Then we came upon the idea of acquiring land and setting up fixed camps along the river. Now we operate four camps. What was once an intense, expedition-style descent has become a distinctively Patagonia experience taking in a host of activities . . . plus amazing rafting."

Earth Adventures has dubbed the float "the world's wildest, most comfortable river trip."

Your float down the Fu starts with a bang. Not long after put-in, you reach Infierno Canyon and an onslaught of rapids as daunting as Dante in the original Italian. These include *Infierno*, *Purgatorio*, and *Escala de Jacobo* (Jacob's Ladder). Fortunately, paddlers have had a day of training to prepare for this trial by fire: "Many guests look upon the river at the first descent and exclaim, 'My God, we're not going to run this!'" Robert shared. "After you run Infierno, you've got your legs under you. Guests quickly grow together as a team. I love watching their confidence grow. And we have two guides for every three guests; one in the raft, the other in a cataraft in case anyone has a problem. It's true that there's little room for screwing up on a river like the Futaleufú. But I've taken four thousand people down to date, and it always works. If you tell people on a rafting trip you've done the Fu, they're going to put you at the front of the boat. They figure you know what's going on." (Note: The river has an extensive trail system; if you're not up for attempting a certain rapid, you can always walk around it. The trails also afford excellent access for hiking and horseback riding.)

The Futaleufú's white-water challenges are rivaled by Earth River's eclectic camps and the abundance of nonrafting activities available. Cave Camp (the first night's on-river lodging) is situated beneath a massive overhanging slab of white granite and is outfitted with a fireplace, a heart-shaped granite hot tub (courtesy of the Fu), and natural skylights. Here, adventure options include rock climbing up and rappelling down Tower of the Winds, a three-hundred-foot spire, and zip-lining across the Zeta Rapid, a Class VI cascade that adjoins camp. The water is so clear in the pools below Zeta that you can spy gargantuan brown trout—up to thirty pounds—finning near the bottom. (Given this, it's no surprise that Fu is also renowned for its fly-fishing.) After the crossing, you'll hike several hours up to the Tree Camp, where eight interconnected, hexagon-shaped tree houses

OPPOSITE:
With more than thirty Class IV and V rapids, the Futaleufú is considered one of the world's top white-water venues.

resting in old growth will be home. The Tree Camp affords some excellent views of snow-capped mountains, two glacier lakes, and the Fu down below. Andean condors are frequently spotted soaring the thermals.

After more hiking, swimming, and an afternoon of canyoneering, Futaleufú adventurers arrive at what Robert called the largest day of white water in the world. "All week, we've been engaging in a form of team building, building trust so everything can work," he continued. "It's immediately put to the test in Terminator, one of the hardest commercially run rapids anywhere. You have to make many technical moves as if in a creek, but it's a huge river. You have to put the boat precisely where it needs to be. The next mile and a half is nonstop Class V. There's the Himalayas—with huge fifteen-foot waves—then *el Cojín* and *Mundaca*." After a "calm" series of Class IV water and lunch, there are two more Class Vs, *Mas o Menos* and *Casa de Piedra*. "Casa Piedra may be the largest rapid on the river. But by the time we run this rapid, the team is solid, and you know you can play this game." The day ends with a traditional Chilean *asado* of barbequed lamb.

"When we arrived at the Futaleufú in the early nineties, the local people looked at us like we were nuts," Robert recalled. "Their opinion slowly evolved as the years went by and we brought tourists into the area who contributed to the economy. Now, many of their children are river guides, and they've traveled all over the world. There's even a university that teaches a program in adventure travel.

"The Chilean government (along with the Spanish power company Endesa) has proposed a hydroelectric project that would place three dams on the Futaleufú. When this proposal surfaced, we took a group of local people up to the town of Santa Barbara where the famed Bìo-Bìo had been dammed. Jobs had been promised to the local people, but it didn't work out that way. All outside workers were brought in, and once the dam was finished, the commerce was done. Some Santa Barbara residents shared their story with our group. By the time we got back to the Futaleufú, the people were in tears."

As of this writing, the future of the Futaleufú is still undetermined.

ROBERT CURRIE has been a partner with Earth River Expeditions since 1992 and leads most of Earth River's trips. He has rafted on five continents and is one of the most experienced river guides in South America. Robert has led first descents on Chile's Futaleufú, Peru's Yavero, and China's Poe Sang Poe. He has been featured in *Outside* magazine, *Town & Country*, *National Geographic Adventure*, and the *New York Times*. Robert started the Earth River Land Trust on the Futaleufú in 1995, which has preserved more than twelve miles of very developable, irreplaceable river. Working with the Chilean government, he was instrumental in bringing protection to Chile and Patagonia from waterborne invasive species that adversely impact rivers, streams, and lakes, destroying fisheries and tourism. Robert lives in Santiago, Chile, with his wife, Maria Luisa. (You can check on the status of the Futaleufú at www.futaleufuriverkeeper.org.)

If You Go

▶ **Getting There:** Trips begin and end in Puerto Montt, which is served by LAN (866-435-9526; www.lan.com) via Santiago.

▶ **Best Time to Visit:** The austral summer: December through mid-April.

▶ **Guides/Outfitters:** Earth River (800-643-2784; www.earthriver.com) pioneered commercial rafting trips on the Futaleufú.

▶ **Level of Difficulty:** Less seasoned paddlers in good condition can tackle the Fu with the help of Earth River's expert guides.

▶ **Accommodations:** For the nights before and after your river sojourn, Earth River recommends the Hotel Cumbres Puerro Varas (+65 2 222 000; www.cumbrespuertovaras .cl) in Puerto Varas (near Puerto Montt).

11

DESTINATION

GALÁPAGOS

RECOMMENDED BY **Morag Prosser**

"The Galápagos is a place where you'll have life-changing moments," Morag Prosser declared. "The environment is like nowhere else, and you can have incredible up-close and personal contact with wildlife—be it a shark swimming alongside your kayak or a ray breaching in front of you or blue-footed boobies fighting for fish above your head. Many people experience the Galápagos from yachts that must moor out in deeper water. With our kayak excursion, we can see it from close to shore. The water is so crystal clear, it's like snorkeling from a boat . . . though there are plenty of opportunities for real snorkeling, too."

Mention Galápagos and many images come to mind—giant turtles, sea lions, iguanas, and, of course, the specter of a bearded Charles Darwin, scribbling furiously in a notebook. The first recorded mention of the sixty-one islands that comprise the Galápagos—only thirteen of which are of considerable size—was recorded in 1535 by the bishop of Panama, Tomás de Berlanga. The islands seemed so dry and uninhabitable that he didn't even bother to name them, though he did make note of the "galapagos," or giant tortoises, that he encountered there. For the next three hundred years or so, sealers, whalers, and assorted buccaneers used the Galápagos as an occasional base of operations, slaughtering legions of sea turtles for meat. By the time Darwin arrived in 1835, the islands' only permanent human residents were members of a penal colony established by the Ecuadorian government on the island of Floreana.

Evolution enthusiasts aside, the great attraction of the Galápagos is the odd and wonderful assemblage of fauna that call the islands home. Penguins. Finches. Pink flamingos. Galápagos sea lions (a sub species of the California sea lion). Sea turtles. Tortoises. Fur seals. The eclectic array of animal life on this small archipelago six hundred miles off

OPPOSITE:
Galápagos
paddlers will
find fascinating
animal life
on both water
and land.

DESTINATION

12

the coast of Ecuador begs the question, "How did they get here . . . and why?" Scientists believe that the Galápagos were created from volcanic activity on the ocean floor, and that they've never been connected to a continent. All its resident animals arrived on the islands by swimming (seals dolphins, penguins), floating (tortoises, iguanas, insects, some plants), or flying (birds, seeds floating in air currents) from as far afield as the Caribbean and the Antarctic. The "why" is a bit of a harder question to answer, though the fact that two important ocean currents—the southern Humboldt Current and northern Panama Current—flow near the Galápagos certainly facilitated and influenced the animals' passage. Once there, the animals were able to adapt and survive—despite the unbalanced assortment of species—thanks to the absence of predators, with the exception of man.

Over time, special efforts have been taken to minimize the footprint mankind leaves on the Galápagos. In 1959—the hundredth anniversary of the publication of Darwin's masterwork—the archipelago was declared a national park; it would later become a UNESCO World Heritage Site. "Visitor activities in the Galápagos are quite controlled," Morag continued, "and there are many rules. But we're able to spend several days on the islands, and that gives us more of a chance to get off the main tourist routes. It also helps support the local economy." One of the early highlights of a Galápagos kayaking adventure comes shortly after stepping off the plane. "After being briefed on park and animal viewing protocol, we hop in our kayaks and head out of town to a secluded beach camp," Morag said. "When you get to your tent, your only other neighbors are marine iguanas, sea lions, turtles, and blue-footed boobies. You might look out your tent and find turtles burying their eggs in the sand or see a hundred marine iguanas all piled up, soaking in the sun. There are no other human visitors around besides our group, despite the fact that the islands are one of the busiest ecotourist destinations on earth."

On her kayaking excursion around the Galápagos, Morag visited five islands. (Kayaks are not used to get from place to place but instead provide a way to get a unique perspective on the island's wildlife; an average kayak excursion involves two to three hours of paddling.) Morag shared a few of her favorite experiences. "I loved visiting Kicker Rock [off the island of San Cristóbal]. This is where many sharks—reef and white tips—hang out. They stand out distinctly against the white-sand bottom. As you're snorkeling above, they eventually drift up. I also saw giant eagle rays, dolphins, and a hammerhead shark there. Los Tuneles is another awe-inspiring site, a short distance off Isla Isabela. This rock formation, with natural arches, was formed when volcanic lava hit the water. You can walk on the lava rock and watch sharks and sea lions in the lagoon. I found myself marveling at the forces of nature that created this little island and at the abundance of sea life.

"My most inspiring experience on the Galápagos came at Isla Lobos, which is home to many juvenile sea lions. There's a lagoon there where the water is quite warm and shallow, and you can swim with the young sea lions. They seem to just want to have fun and share their energy. It's still the most incredible wildlife experience I've ever had. I laughed so much while swimming with them, I must have swallowed a gallon of seawater."

MORAG PROSSER participated in the first commercial descent of the White Nile in Uganda, has skydived in New Zealand, trekked the Golden Triangle in Thailand, and trucked across Iceland . . . among many other adventures. Morag has a law degree from the University of Aberdeen, but when she moved to Idaho, she sought a more adventurous career and now works as a ROW Adventures consultant and international trip specialist. She resides in Coeur d'Alene, with her husband and three dogs and doesn't let any moss grow under her feet.

If You Go

▶ **Getting There:** Travelers stage in Guayaquil and, from there, fly to San Cristóbal in the Galápagos. Guayaquil is served from Miami by a number of carriers, including LAN Ecuador (866-435-9526; www.lan.com) and Copa Airlines (800-359-2672; www.copaair.com). Tame (www.tame.com.ec) offers flights to San Cristóbal.

▶ **Best Time to Visit:** You can dive in the Galápagos year-round, though the high season is considered November to April, July, and August.

▶ **Level of Difficulty:** Beginner paddlers will have no trouble with this trip.

▶ **Guides/Outfitters:** A number of companies lead trips to the Galápagos, though ROW Adventures' (800-451-6034; www.rowadventures.com) land-based trip is unique.

▶ **Accommodations:** Lodging includes a mix of camping and island hotels.

DESTINATION 12

UPPER NAVUA RIVER

RECOMMENDED BY **George Wendt**

When George Wendt began looking for new places to take rafters, Fiji was not even on his mental map. "From 1974 to '91, I was part owner of a company called Sobek [Mountain Travel] that ran river trips among its other excursions," George began. "One of our early international destinations was the Omo River in Ethiopia. We'd pore over maps, trying to identify new places that would be good travel destinations. We looked at Tahiti and Hawaii, but they weren't right. It never entered my mind that Fiji might have any rafting that was worthwhile, let alone a river that flowed twelve months of the year. In 1997, we learned of a river in Fiji. One of my associates went, and when he came back, I asked him how the river—the Upper Navua—was. He said it was 'pretty good.' He shared six photographs. 'Pretty good?' I exclaimed. 'It's BEAUTIFUL!'

"The following year, I went over to see for myself. It seemed like the perfect river: an enthralling canyon; a narrow gorge, in some places just twenty feet wide, with towering walls of lava and limestone framed by a canopy of emerald green. Despite how the river narrowed, there were no precipitous drops; at that time, it was all Class II. 'We're floating through a tropical paradise without any worry of going over a waterfall,' I thought. It's the most idyllic river experience I could imagine."

Fiji is a nation of over 330 islands in the South Pacific region of Melanesia, some 1,300 miles northeast of New Zealand's North Island. Many may not realize that Fiji, celebrated for its white sandy beaches and warm, clear water, is also home to remote rainforest highlands . . . particularly on Viti Levu, the archipelago's largest island. Here, at the island's core, lush forests encircle Mount Tomanivi (which tops out at over 4,500 feet), and jungle rains feed the Upper Navua. The river flows a total of forty miles; the gorge section is roughly eighteen miles long. "After my trip down the river, I realized it was something

OPPOSITE:
In places, the
Upper Navua
narrows to less
than twenty feet
in width, with
walls climbing
to one hundred
and fifty feet.

very special and that others would enjoy it as much as I had," George continued. "We met with the villagers to see if they'd be receptive to the idea of commercial trips being run on the river. They were, but they wanted to know how they would benefit. In 2000, we brought all the parties to the table—nine landowning clans, two villages, a logging company, and the Native Land Trust board—and came up with a plan that would be more economically beneficial to the community than logging. We would lease the upper river canyon for twenty-five years, and the lumber company would do no logging within two hundred meters of either side of the river. We would train younger men in the community to be river guides so they could have year-round employment, and we'd pay the local landowners a fee for each person we took down the river. Thus far, over $600,000 has been paid to landowners from rafters."

Upper Navua expeditions begin on the coast in Pacific Harbor. From here, it's an hour and a half to the put-in, with rests at an elevation of nearly two thousand feet. "We like to have the bus stop about halfway up," George said. "It's a chance to stretch and use the restroom. Before we get back in the bus, I ask people to take ninety seconds and be silent and simply listen. You can hear birds off in the distance, the gentle rustling of the wind, and the movement of water. The voyage of discovery begins. Once we put in on the river, it continues. We run it in four- to six-passenger rafts; the guide in the back has oars. (A slide put some rocks in the river a few years back and now there's a brief Class III section that requires some maneuvering.) For much of the drift, the canyon is bathed in moss, ferns, all manner of tropical greenery. It seems as if you're floating through an orchid plantation. It's not too hot, in the seventies or eighties; even if it rains a bit, the water is warm and the conditions are still comfortable. You pass many waterfalls en route, eighty to a hundred. Some are just trickles off the canyon walls; others are quite significant. If you visit in the rainy season, there might be two hundred waterfalls. There are a few places where you can step under a waterfall and get a 'free' massage. I think my favorite section is where the canyon really tightens up. For three miles, it's only 18 to 25 feet wide, and the walls climb 100 to 150 feet. As you float silently through, it's a great chance to be aware of the sights and smells, to really take in a special environment."

George summed it up simply: If cost is not a limiting factor, you should visit Fiji if only to do this river trip. It may be the best in the world.

"I happened to be on the Upper Navua in 2002 when the Eco-Challenge was being held in Fiji," George recalled. [*Eco-Challenge* was a televised race involving mixed-sex teams racing nonstop over a three-hundred-mile course, involving various disciplines, including trekking, kayaking, mountain biking, and mountaineering.] "A key part of the course involved floating down this section of the river. The first thirteen teams came through on day one, another forty teams on day two. I slept in the gorge on the night of day two, as I wanted to be there at dawn when the last of the teams came through. I could hear their voices before I could see them. 'This is amazing,' they were saying. 'I've never seen anything remotely as beautiful as this.' These teams had no chance of winning, and they were extremely tired. Yet even in their exhaustion, they were filled with wonderment at the beauty of the canyon."

GEORGE WENDT is the founder and president of O.A.R.S. "My first trip in the Grand Canyon introduced me to a world that I didn't know existed," he once said. He soon left his life as a middle school math teacher and began leading people onto the world's waterways. Since forming O.A.R.S. in 1972, George has directly (or indirectly) taken half a million people on water adventures. Originally, O.A.R.S. focused on rivers in the American west. Today, the company also leads trips in Alaska, western Canada, Latin America, and Fiji. In 2006, George received a Lifetime Achievement Award from the Adventure Travel Trade Association for his pioneering efforts in the realms of white-water rafting, ecotourism, and adventure travel.

If You Go

▶ **Getting There:** A number of carriers serve Fiji, including Fiji Airways (800-227-4446; www.fijiairways.com), which offers flights from Los Angeles.
▶ **Best Time to Visit:** River trips are run year-round on the Upper Navua. Wetter weather occurs December through March, though even then, temperatures are mild.
▶ **Guides/Outfitters:** Rivers Fiji (209-736-0597; www.riversfiji.com), which is affiliated with O.A.R.S., leads day trips on both Upper Navua and Luva Rivers.
▶ **Level of Difficulty:** Guided trips require no previous paddling experience.
▶ **Accommodations:** O.A.R.S. recommends the Pearl (+679 773 0022; www.thepearl southpacific.com) in Pacific Harbor. Tourism Fiji (www.fiji.travel) lists other lodging options.

FLORIDA KEYS

RECOMMENDED BY **Captain Bill Keogh**

"Some years ago, one of the tourism development councils down in the Keys came up with a slogan—'It's the Bahamas that you can drive to,'" Bill Keogh recalled. "I think that covers it pretty well. If you went to the Bahamas or some other Caribbean island, you'd find the same sort of ecosystem; the warm, clear water; the sand flats. For some people, it's a lot more comfortable to stay in the U.S. to experience this sort of ecosystem."

While technically part of Florida and the United States, the Keys have always stood somewhat apart, dancing to the beat of their own free-spirited drum. The more than 1,700 islands that make up the archipelago stretch 110 miles from Key Largo in the northeast to Key West in the southwest, though only 43 of the islands are connected by bridges. Each of the main islands has its own persona and attractions. Key Largo attracts many divers; Islamorada is a sportfishing Mecca; Big Pine Key is the very definition of laid back; and Key West, the end of the road (and most southerly point in the continental United States), draws revelers, artists, and one major sailing regatta.

Bill's impetus to explore the Keys was simple: snow, or the lack of it. "I grew up in Connecticut and went to college in Maine, where I pursued a photography minor," he said. "One day, I saw a posting in the photo lab that read 'Spend your winters in Florida.' That sounded pretty good, and I applied for the job . . . and got it. I ran the photo department for a research station. It was the perfect platform to explore the Keys, as there was a full staff of scientists on board to help me learn about the region. At one point, I did some photography work for Ocean Kayak. One of the outfitters in the area saw my photos and asked if I would be interested in trading some photo work for kayaks. I said, 'No thanks, I've got some canoes.' He eventually convinced me, and I took some. Pretty soon I had a little fleet and started doing ecotours. Given the water orientation of the Keys, its

OPPOSITE:

Healthy mangrove habitat and clear water make the Florida Keys a great place to view marine life from your kayak.

residents have a lot of boats—something like thirty thousand or forty thousand for a population of eighty thousand. The smart folks have a kayak. Craft that don't draw much water give you the best way to explore."

Bill calls Big Pine Key home, and from here has easy access to all the elements of the Florida Keys ecosystem—mangroves, hardwood hammocks, shallow-water sea grass, shallow-water sponge flats, coral reef, and beaches. "One of my favorite paddles goes to No Name Key," Bill continued. "It's only a ten-minute paddle to reach No Name, and once there, you're out of the wind. There's a creek that runs through the mangroves. We line up in single file and enter this primitive, red mangrove forest. The canopy gives this spot a real tropical atmosphere, almost like you're hiking the woods. It's quite narrow, and you're paddling with half a paddle, pulling yourself through by the roots. As you tune into the atmosphere, you can start to pick out all this life in the submerged mangrove roots that hang down like fingers into the water. There are mollies, needlefish, baby tarpon, mangrove snapper, grouper, sea stars, brittle stars, echinoderms, sea squirts, anemones, clams, oysters, and hermit crabs, all living in the root systems. Soon you come to interior salt lakes, which are home to a great deal of bird life—flamingos, ibis and other wading birds, as well as raptors like ospreys and bald eagles. When you come back into the mangroves again, your eyes are adjusted to the light, and you'll pick up more critters. When we come out by the No Name Key Bridge, there's a chance we'll see manatee or spotted eagle rays. Sometimes the rays will jump out of the water, which is something to see."

If Bill wants to cover more ground, he might drop a few kayaks in his motorboat. "Having the boat lets you cover a lot more miles of backcountry," he continued. "Instead of two or three miles, you might cover six, ten, or twelve. You get to the kind of remote areas you might only see with a flats fishing guide. As we're making our way to the spot where we're going to drop the kayaks, people have a chance to view the water from a higher aspect. You can see turtles, stingrays, sharks, and manatee. It gets you jazzed up and ready to jump in the kayak. Where I'll go with the boat will depend on what people want to see—a good bird island, for example, or a spot where you're pretty sure to see turtles. Some people want to go fishing. I can take fly anglers to flats where we can look for bonefish or permit or tarpon. Or we can troll little poppers or a jig over grass flats on the edge of the Gulf. Here, you'll pick up sea trout, jack crevalle, small grouper, ladyfish— you're never sure what you'll get. It's very exciting to have a ladyfish jump six times right in front of you. We even take the kayaks out to free dive for spiny lobsters."

The fertile waters of the Florida Keys are so teeming with life that you never know quite what you'll see. One June, Bill looked onto the flats near his home to see mating nurse sharks. "It was a full moon, and I could hear this occasional splashing. I got in my kayak and paddled out to find these big nurse sharks—eleven feet long—in knee-deep water. The males would suck down on the pectoral fins of the females to hold them in place—the suction sound was very audible—then they'd twist and copulate, tails thrashing. I paddled out every night for two weeks to watch this display.

"A few weeks later, I could see ten-inch nurse sharks in the grass. The moms weren't far away, but they were getting ready to make new babies."

CAPTAIN BILL KEOGH has lived in the lower Keys for more than two decades and has made his living on or in these waters as a naturalist guide, educator, and professional photographer. He has been published in numerous books, magazines, and publications throughout the world and coproduced *The Florida Keys: The Natural Wonders of an Island Paradise* by Jeff Ripple. He's the author of *The Florida Keys Paddling Guide,* and his photos have been used by *National Geographic,* the Nature Conservancy, World Wildlife Fund, Florida Keys National Wildlife Refuges, among others.

If You Go

▶ **Getting There:** Most visitors will fly to Miami, which is served by most major air carriers. From here, it's 130 miles to Big Pine Key.

▶ **Best Time to Visit:** Temperatures are clement year-round, though the Keys see a bit more rain in the late spring and summer—and in early fall, there's the greatest potential for bigger storms.

▶ **Guides/Outfitters:** Many outfitters serve the Keys area, including Big Pine Kayak Adventures (305-872-7474; www.keyskayaktours.com).

▶ **Level of Difficulty:** Beginners will be fine in the more sheltered areas, though if you head out on more open water, the wind can come up fast.

▶ **Accommodations:** Visit Florida (www.visitflorida.com) highlights many lodging options in the Keys.

14

DESTINATION

CRETE (THE SOUTH COAST)

RECOMMENDED BY **Keith Heger**

"I first learned of the southern coast of Crete from my boss, Rick Sweitzer," Keith Heger began. "Rick had visited in the early seventies. He found himself in Matala, where a number of hippies and musicians were hanging out, including Joni Mitchell. [Matala was immortalized in the song "Carey" from Mitchell's classic album, *Blue*.] He felt a connection with the Minoan people, and when he launched Northwest Passage in the early nineties, he returned. Initially he led bike trips, but when kayaking began gaining in popularity, he started exploring the possibilities . . . and ended up assembling what's become our most popular trip. In terms of history, scenery, hospitality, and overall paddling experience, I think the stretch of coast from Roumeli to Matala highlights some of the best that the Mediterranean has to offer.

"Internally, we call it the 'Magical Minoan Mystery Tour.'"

Crete sits 100 miles southeast of the tip of mainland Greece. It's the largest of the Greek Isles, stretching 160 miles from east to west, and was home to Europe's earliest-known civilization, the Minoans. The tour that Keith loves to lead begins in Matala and explores some of the caves that the flower children once populated. "We run south from town toward a spot called Red Beach," he detailed, "and en route, we come to the most amazing sea caves. They are like cathedrals within the rock, the sandstone bleached almost white. Many of the caves rest in little slots; you'd never notice them if you weren't looking for them. There's one cave that's very large, a big arcing space. It's completely dark, and you can hear the bats above. If you poke farther back, there's a narrow slot, no wider than your kayak. This leads to another cavern, large enough to hold eight kayaks and a little beach. If you turn off your headlamp, there's not an inch of light, just the sound of the bats and water sloshing about. It's like solving a Rubik's Cube to get the boats all facing in the right direction to exit, but it's worth it. If I'm with a group, we'll head on to Red Beach and Kommos Beach (where there are some fine Minoan ruins) and then turn back. If I'm on my own, I might continue around the point and then east on to Lentas. You're paddling against sheer rock walls, past little beaches, and even olive groves. It's an unreal stretch of coast."

After exploring the caves near Matala, you'll hop in a car and drive west to take in the Samaria Gorge, Europe's longest gorge. "For many guests, the ten-mile hike into the gorge is a highlight of the trip," Keith continued. "The gorge sees many visitors, but nearly all of them must catch the ferry from Agia Roumeli in the late afternoon. We stay in Roumeli, and thus we don't have to deal with the mobs." After waking in a seaside inn to the sound of bells from herds of goats on the hillside, you'll begin the paddle back to Matala. "You get a 180-degree view of the Samaria Gorge from the water as you paddle by," Keith said. "The light in the early morning is wonderful. The green hillsides and the blue waters change as the day goes on. In a few miles we come to Agios Pavlos and stop in for a cappuccino. There's a small chapel here built in the tenth century in honor of St. Paul. [Some believe he was shipwrecked along the coast here as he was being returned to Rome from Jerusalem to face trial.] Marmara Beach is the next stop, one of the nicest lunch spots on the trip. There are marble bluffs left and right, the kind of marble you could imagine in your bathroom. We stay in Loutro that night. Entering the bay is enthralling. You come around a big point, and the first thing you see is a whitewashed house. A few more paddle strokes and the village of blue and white buildings appears. It's a treat. Often, we'll bob a few minutes, just taking in the view."

After a layover in Loutro, where there's the option to paddle back to Marmara Beach or to Sweetwater Beach (where freshwater springs trickle into the sea), comes a big day— twenty miles. It sounds daunting, but it's split into several sessions. "The mountains pull back a bit here, and farmland is closer to the water," Keith continued. "There's some great water to paddle in this stretch. There are rock gardens that you can weave around; you'll often find sea turtles in this area. Our destination is Plakias, one of the larger towns in the region. You can see it in the distance, and it seems far away. On this final stretch of the day, the west wind will sometimes come up. It creates six- to eight-foot swells, and the waves will take you right into town. You're flying along without any paddle strokes, just steering. It's a chance to develop some new paddling skills. Everyone is pretty salty and tired after this day. A shower feels great!"

15

DESTINATION

Your last full day is another big one—eighteen miles if you forego the optional shuttle at the end. "You can shave off a little at the beginning," Keith offered, "by cutting through a beautiful sunlit cave. It's Crete's own Grotta Azzurra—like the one on Capri without the crowds or an entry fee. We pass Palm Beach, a freshwater estuary lined with palm trees at the base of Preveli Monastery. We continue on to Triopetra Beach, where we'll take a lunch break. After Triopetra, the shoreline takes a turn. There's a lot of exposure here. It's an exciting place to paddle, even on the calmest day. In the distance, you can make out some of the landmarks around Matala from the first day. People have to dig deep to make the last five miles to Agia Galini, our stop for the night. We have dinner on the third floor of a tavern, with the lights of Timbaki and Matala flickering before us. You can sleep in and drive to Matala the next morning or do an eight-mile open-water paddle. Doing the paddle gives people a great sense of accomplishment."

KEITH HEGER is program director, guide, and instructor with Northwest Passage. A Chicago-area native, his adventures have taken him around the world—to North, South, and Central America; Western Europe; the Mediterranean; Antarctica; and the Arctic. Keith is well versed in the skills of wilderness travel and group leadership. Outdoor interests include sea kayaking, white-water kayaking, rafting, canoeing, skiing, snowboarding, rock climbing, mountaineering, and sailing.

If You Go

▶ **Getting There:** Trips stage in Heraklion, the capital of Crete, which can be reached from Athens via Olympic Air (+30 210 3550500; www.olympicair.com) or Aegean Airlines (+30 210 6261000; www.aegeanair.com).

▶ **Best Time to Visit:** Mid-May through September is the prime time for kayaking.

▶ **Guides/Outfitters:** Several outfitters serve Crete, including Northwest Passage (800-256-4409; www.nwpassage.com) and Enjoy Crete (+30.6946140777; www.enjoy-crete.com).

▶ **Level of Difficulty:** Visitors don't need prior kayaking experience, though they should be in good physical shape, as there are a few long paddling days.

▶ **Accommodations:** The Hellenic Chamber of Hotels (www.grhotels.gr) lists many options for both Athens and Heraklion.

OPPOSITE:
A variety of sea caves punctuate the south coast of Crete.

DESTINATION 15

MILOS

RECOMMENDED BY **Rod Feldtmann**

"I first came to Milos as a geologist, to work on a gold mining project," Rod Feldtmann began. "I fell in love with a local girl, got married, and fell in love with the island. As the geology project began to wind down, I realized that I had to either make something up to sustain my existence or go elsewhere to find work. Earlier, I'd bought a kayak and paddled around the island. I saw Milos's great potential as a kayaking destination and ended up buying a few more boats and starting a business. As a geologist, I could really appreciate the island's incredibly varied coastline, the product of a million years of volcanic eruptions. You have a tremendous variety of different rock types here; every headland and bay is different in that sense. It's not just long stretches of spectacular cliffs or extensive beaches. There's a mix, all united by turquoise blue waters."

Milos rests in the Aegean Sea, between the southern tip of mainland Greece and the island of Crete; it's the southwesternmost island in the Cyclades group, home of two better-known vacation retreats, Santorini and Mykonos. The island was an important source of obsidian for the region in the time before bronze supplanted it as a weapons material, and it was here that a statue of the goddess Aphrodite was discovered, better known as the Venus de Milo. "Milos is perfect as a base for kayakers," Rod continued. "It's big enough to offer over twelve different day trips, but small enough that I can drive from one side of the island to the other in less than half an hour so we can always be sheltered from the wind. The day is spent paddling, not driving."

A typical day on the azure waters off Milos is taken at a leisurely pace, entailing three hours of paddling and plenty of stops for snorkeling, sunning at isolated beaches, and even some cliff jumping. Rod discussed a few of his favorite outings. "There are sea caves all around the island, but there's a concentration of them along the southwestern coast,

OPPOSITE:
"The Bears"—
a distinctive rock
formation at
the entrance to the
harbor of Milos.

at a place called Kleftiko, a spectacular complex of high cliffs, sea passages, tunnels, and arches. The name is taken from the Greek word *kleftes*, meaning thief, as local legend says Kleftiko was a popular haven for pirates in the Middle Ages. [Kleftiko's freestanding arch is frequently featured in Greece's promotional literature.]

"Another paddle that we enjoy is across to the island of Kimolos, the next island north. It's only a one-kilometer crossing from our starting point at Apollonia Bay, which takes about fifteen minutes. Kimolos is very rugged, and there's no road access to the west coast. Here, there are numerous fascinating rock formations fashioned from volcanic lavas, including sea stacks stuck up like pinnacles and caves so deep that torch lights are required for exploration. The hillsides are covered with stone terraces, which were origi-nally built in ancient times to retain soil and water for farming. There's a nice hike from the lunch-stop beach along some of the terraces to see abandoned stone farmhouses with stunning vistas of the Aegean Sea. Kimolos has some nice spots to snorkel, and there are several great rock-jumping locations."

As Rod previously mentioned, the north wind can come up at times. When conditions for the outer coastline are less favorable, he likes to head to the harbor of Milos, which is essentially the crater of the volcano that formed the island. "I like to paddle along the east-ern entrance of the bay," Rod continued. "There are four fishing villages here, each with a small number of houses—a dozen to twenty. The dwellings have boathouses dug into the cliffside with brightly colored doorways. The setting is very picturesque. At the entrance of the harbor there's a distinctive rock formation called the Bears. If I feel that the group I'm with is up for a challenge, I'll take them around this headland. Suddenly you're exposed. Less seasoned paddlers aren't used to the open, rougher water, but most do fine. When we've had enough of the bigger water, we can duck back into the bay for lunch."

If it's windy enough, Rod can put the breezes to his advantage. "I sometimes carry the fly of an old three-man tent with me," he explained. "If the wind is heavy, we raft our kayaks together and tie the fly off the paddles, prop the paddles up, and use the whole setup like a sail. If it's working well, we'll travel faster than I can paddle."

(Note: If you'd prefer an expedition-style trip, a circumnavigation of Milos is possible. It's a paddle of approximately fifty-five miles over five days. Paddlers camp on pristine beaches, with meals prepared by their guide.)

It's no secret that Greece has had its share of economic woes; spend a week in Athens and you have a decent chance of experiencing the inconvenience of a strike of some sort.

But in a rural, off-the-vacation spot like Milos, the vicissitudes of austerity are mostly far removed. Plus, you have an opportunity to see the lives of real Greek islanders on display. "Our base is in the village of Triovasalos, where my wife has a guesthouse and café," Rod said. "It's not a touristy place, though there are over a dozen restaurants within walking distance. Our kayaking program leaves plenty of time to explore them." If you find yourself in the family café in the evening, you may find Rod's father-in-law serving grilled octopus and ouzo. "It's just locals and kayakers," Rod added.

Rod Feldtmann grew up on a farm in Victoria, Australia. After graduating with a degree in geology from the University of Wollongong, he worked for ten years as an exploration geologist in Australia, South America, and finally in Milos. In 2000, when his contract as a geologist came to an end, Rod established Sea Kayak Milos as a means to remain on the island, support his family, and enjoy the great outdoors. With fourteen years' experience leading trips on Milos and to other places in Greece, he is one of the most experienced and qualified guides in Greece. He regularly travels to the U.K. to attend British Canoe Union (BCU) training courses. He holds his five-star sea kayak proficiency certificate and is a BCU Level 4 sea kayak coach.

If You Go

▶ **Getting There:** Visitors can reach Milos on Olympic Air (+30 210 3550500; www .olympicair.com) from Athens, which is served by many carriers.

▶ **Best Time to Visit:** April to October is prime time for kayaking trips around Milos. Guided circumnavigation trips are generally led in June and October.

▶ **Guides/Outfitters:** Sea Kayak Milos (+30 228 7023597; www.seakayakgreece.com) leads day trips and seasonal circumnavigations. Northwest Passage (800-256-4409; www.nwpassage.com) also leads circumnavigations.

▶ **Level of Difficulty:** Visitors to Milos do not need advanced kayaking skills.

▶ **Accommodations:** Sea Kayak Milos offers Stay and Paddle packages through Petrinella's Guesthouse in the village of Triovasalos. Other options are listed at www .milostravel.com.

NA PALI COAST

RECOMMENDED BY **Josh Comstock**

The seventeen miles of the Na Pali Coast on Kauai's northwest shore have been called one of the most challenging day paddles in the world. Josh Comstock simply calls it home.

"Water has always been part of my life, whether it's surfing, river kayaking, or outrigger racing," he began. "After living in Santa Cruz, Newport Beach, and Oahu, I landed in Kauai near the Na Pali Coast. It's such an intriguing area with such a rich history. It was the first place in the Hawaiian chain that the Marquesans settled. It is also the oldest island in the chain. Kauai has a very powerful *mana* (life force). It's very evident when you paddle the Na Pali. The scenery is tremendous, but when you know a little about the area's history, it's mind-blowing. You feel a connection to that history when you're paddling."

Kauai is known—at least in promotional literature—as the "Garden Isle." As it turns out, these travel brochures speak the truth. Kauai's defining physical characteristic is Mount Waialeale, a volcanic peak that rises from the center of this mountainous island. While not Kauai's highest mountain, Mount Waialeale is responsible for capturing the moisture that makes the central part of the island one of the wettest places on earth, with an average annual rainfall of 476 inches. In addition to supplementing Kauai's rich flora, eons of rain have created some incredibly dramatic canyon landscapes, including Waimea Canyon, which Mark Twain once dubbed "the Grand Canyon of the Pacific," and, of course, the fabulous fluted cliffsides of the Na Pali Coast. Some of the cliffs rise four thousand feet. Many are festooned with lush, tropical greenery and topped by wisps of clouds and mist, a setting that fosters a mystical aura.

Josh vividly recalls his first paddle along the Na Pali. "I was already a pretty experienced paddler when I arrived on Kauai and thought that I could figure it out myself. I got in a situation within a half hour of being out on the water. It can get very windy out there, and

OPPOSITE:

The seventeen-mile stretch of the Na Pali Coast that paddlers navigate is more a test of endurance than of paddling expertise.

that first day it was blowing thirty-five miles per hour. My boat flipped over. It was a sit-on-top kayak and started floating away pretty quickly. The boat and the paddle got separated, and for a second I was torn about which direction to swim. Fortunately, I remembered that I had an extra paddle in the boat. I was immediately humbled. The waters off Na Pali are rough. You have to be on your game out there; it's not to be taken lightly."

This being said, the Na Pali Coast paddle—generally seven hours—is not just for seasoned kayakers. "Most people think that a seventeen-mile paddle is not vacation material," Josh added. "The people who think it's an awesome idea, those are the people who go and enjoy it. The paddle offers both physical and mental challenges. We have guests who have never been in a kayak do this trip every day. If you live an active lifestyle, you can do it. When people call to book a day on the water, I give them a primer that includes worst-case scenarios. This kind of screening means that the people who show up at the shop in the morning are people who should be there."

Na Pali paddlers begin at Haena Beach and head in a southwesterly direction, finally taking out seventeen miles later at Polihale State Park. "We stop every twenty minutes or so to take in the views or discuss some historical aspect of what we're seeing," Josh continued. "The first stop comes just after we come into the open water, as we pass Ke'e Beach. There's a shrine at Ke'e Beach in honor of the goddess of Hula, and there's a hula school; it's one of Hawaii's most sacred places. There was no written language in the old days; hula was a way to tell stories through dancing and chanting. Some people will get seasick with the waves, and if that's the case, we encourage them to head back in at this point. (We recommend that guests use a Dramamine patch.) If everyone is thumbs up/pinkies down, we continue out in our two-person boats. We might come upon green sea turtles as we continue on, maybe monk seals, or a pod of spinner dolphins. Sometimes the dolphins will stay by us for an hour; it's an out-of-body experience.

"Soon we reach Hanakapiai, where there's a series of sea caves. If it's calm enough, we can paddle in. There is a waterfall in front of you that you can opt to paddle through. I recall one morning there when the sun was just coming up, and mist from the waves was hitting the rocks. The soft morning sun was hitting the waterfall as the wind was sweeping the cascading water along in swirls and twists. Another cave has a double door, so you can go in one side and come out the other. As we move south and west, we come into Kauai's rain shadow. As the climate becomes drier, the plant life changes. By the end of the day, we're in the desert. We pass the Kalalau and Honopu Valleys, and finally, after five hours of paddling, we stop for lunch at Milolii Beach. After a swim or a hike to a nearby waterfall, it's back in the kayak for the last two hours. In the afternoon, we'll often see some good tailwinds, which generate waves. We can show people how to surf in their kayaks. You have to learn to stay upright, brace, and steer. But once you get it, people really enjoy it. We also prep guests on how to do surf landings, a nice exclamation point at the end of the paddle.

"By the time we reach Polihale, everyone is pretty tired. Sometimes we [begin the trip with] people who are uncomfortable with the ocean. By the time they've finished the paddle, they've overcome it. Paddling is a way for us to reconnect with the water, an element that's part of us all."

JOSH COMSTOCK paddled into Anahola Kaua'i in 1993 to help build the family farm. In addition to getting down and dirty, he's an experienced leader. Josh has been guiding on the Na Pali Coast for more than seventeen years. After studying Hawaiian history, language, and plant medicine in college, guiding was a natural fit. He worked his way up the not-so-corporate ladder from guide to owner of Na Pali Kayak in 2002. During the off-season, Josh can be found playing in the surf with his daughter, Tallulah, surfing large winter swells, traveling the globe, or helping out on the farm.

If You Go

► **Getting There:** Kauai is served by many carriers, generally through connecting flights from Honolulu or Maui. Direct flights from Los Angeles and San Francisco to Lihue are available on United Airlines (800-864-8331; www.united.com) and American Airlines (800-321-2121; www.aa.com).

► **Best Time to Visit:** Mid-April to early October offers the most consistent conditions.

► **Guides/Outfitters:** Napali Kayak (808-826-6900; www.napalikayak.com) leads day trips along the Na Pali Coast.

► **Level of Difficulty:** Visitors should be fit and active but needn't be expert paddlers.

► **Accommodations:** The Kauai Visitors Bureau (800-262-1400; www.gohawaii.com) provides a comprehensive listing of lodging on the Garden Isle.

RÍO PLÁTANO

RECOMMENDED BY **Dr. Christopher Begley**

The Mosquito Coast is the title of a fine novel by Paul Theroux that involves an alienated Massachusetts man who moves his family to a Central American rainforest for a simpler life. Things did not go well for the fictional family (nor for the novel's translation to the big screen). With the crack team that the Mesoamerican Ecotourism Alliance has assembled—including archeologist Dr. Christopher Begley, naturalist Robert Gallardo, and lead guide Jorge Salaverri—you're likely to have a rewarding adventure and happy denouement as you make your way down Río Plátano, which runs through the seldom-traveled wilderness of northeastern Honduras.

"Some people think of La Mosquitia as a miniature Amazon," Christopher Begley began. "One reason for this comparison is that the Río Plátano Biosphere Reserve is the largest piece of intact rainforest habitat (two million acres) outside of the Amazon. Another reason is the sense of scale that you get here. The Amazon is so big that, in some ways, it's hard to feel a connection. You feel like an observer, rather than a part of it. On the Mosquito Coast, the hilly terrain makes the scope more contained. The river is small, appropriately sized to give you a personal connection. That connection is enhanced by our guides, who are members of the local Pech tribes. All of this combines to make you feel like you're right there, melding with this magical place."

For the record, the "Mosquito" of Mosquito Coast references one of the region's indigenous peoples, the Miskito, not the insect.

Your journey into the jungles of La Mosquitia begins on foot with an eleven-mile hike over two days from the frontier village of Bonanza into the interior; pack mules will carry your gear. At the end of day one, you'll reach the headwaters of the Río Plátano, and the first of many archeological sites, El Higerito. The following day, you'll

18

DESTINATION

push along on foot to the raft put-in, pausing along the way to marvel at the petroglyphs and stone monuments at the site of Lancetillal. "What we've learned about the people who lived here between 500 and 1200 AD is that they combined the cultural mores of the people to the south with traits of the Mesoamerican people—the Mayans and Aztecs—who lived to the north," Christopher continued. "They shared traits unlike any other group we've studied."

The next day you'll reach the river and set off into the heart of this vast wilderness area. "Walking through the jungle for a few days before getting on the rafts makes the river portion of the trip that much more exciting," Christopher said. "By the time you've reached the river, you have some familiarity and appreciation of the terrain. You've worked somewhat hard to get here, and now, for the next week, you can sit back and enjoy it. The Pech guides who accompany us share how the local people relate to the river, and this gives us a richer context for our travels."

One of the appeals of floating Río Plátano is the chance to catch glimpses of the many animals that call the jungle home. "When you're walking through the jungle, the animals hear you from a mile away and make themselves scarce," Christopher explained. "When you're floating down [the river], the approach is almost silent, and you come up very close upon the animals, which are drawn to the river to drink." White-faced capuchin and spider monkeys are commonly seen, as well as white-lipped peccary (a species of wild pig), anteaters, sloths, river otters, and five species of toucans. Baird's tapir are frequently encountered as well; these creatures, which are shaped like large pigs and most notable for their short, prehensile snouts, are related to the horse and rhinoceros. "On one trip, the raft in front of mine floated up on a puma," Christopher recalled. "The puma and jaguar are here, as are harpy eagles, but they're seldom seen. Unless there's been hard rain, the water is crystal clear, and there's a great deal of aquatic life, including giant freshwater prawns that almost resemble lobsters."

Days on the river begin with a leisurely hot breakfast of oatmeal or pancakes. As you peer through the thick canopy of foliage that envelops the river, you may spy a chestnut-mandibled toucan or scarlet macaw—or dwell on the thought that there are no human settlements for many miles in any direction. Blue morpho butterflies offer a vibrant, fluttering display of color against the greenery. While not a white-knuckle white-water river, the Río Plátano has enough rapids to keep your blood pumping—particularly El Subterraneo, a mile-long gorge of Class III rapids that requires a brief portage but rewards

18

DESTINATION

your efforts with excellent possibilities of wildlife encounters. "You have to work a bit to get the raft through places, and it can get your adrenaline going," Begley continued, "but our guides know the river well. There are times when you're going down a set of rapids and a spectacular animal appears. You're trying to watch the animal, negotiate the rapids, and take in the rainforest at the same time. It's such a rich, multilayered experience." There's nothing like a river trip to build a hearty appetite, and wayfarers on Río Plátano are well fed. "Dinners are the big meal," Christopher added, "and Jorge is an excellent camp cook. He'll make soups, pastas, and a local dish called *baleadas*, a combination of flour tortillas, beans, and cheese. We often supplement our meals with fresh fish caught from the river."

Sojourners continue to come upon archeological sites for much of the float. One of the most enigmatic for Christopher is an abandoned village that's come to be called Los Metates. "The site has several large grinding stones," he described. "Some may have been used for corn, but others, which have elaborate markings, likely had some symbolic purpose. What's very curious is that in addition to the large stones, there are literally thousands of miniature ones, the metates. These stones fit in your hand. They seem like small effigies of the larger stones, and no one knows their purpose—were they an offering of sorts, or a tax that was paid?" Farther downriver, there are also eerie petroglyphs carved into river rocks at a spot called Walpaulbantara; no one is certain whether these markings served as boundary markers or recounted creation myths.

Near the bottom of the river, you begin to pass settlements of the Garifuna, Pech, and Miskito peoples. "Our guides hail from some of these villages, and we're often invited to visit their houses, and a community party breaks out," Christopher said. "Thanks to the low level of tourism here, there's no stilted 'watch the indigenous folks dance' program. Villagers bring out their drums and start playing and dancing, and there's nothing artificial about it. Often our group will leave, and the party will still be going on."

DR. CHRISTOPHER BEGLEY is an archaeologist with twenty years' experience in the jungles of Central America. He has been involved in scientific expeditions in the remote Mosquito Coast as well as to urban areas of Central America. Holding a doctorate from the University of Chicago, he has taught archaeology and anthropology and works with issues of tourism and archaeology; Christopher is currently an associate professor of anthropology at Transylvania University in Kentucky. He was a Fulbright Scholar in

El Salvador in 1997. His research has been featured in documentaries on the Discovery Channel, the Travel Channel, and the BBC.

If You Go

▶ **Getting There:** Trips stage in Tegucigalpa, Honduras, which is served by several airlines, including Delta (800-221-1212; www.delta.com) and United Airlines (800-241-6522; www.united.com).

▶ **Best Time to Visit:** Two-week hike-float trips are led in July and August.

▶ **Guides/Outfitters:** Trips are led by the Exploration Foundation (859-608-2478; explorationfoundation.org).

▶ **Level of Difficulty:** Less seasoned rafters will be fine on a guided trip, though they should be prepared for a wilderness experience.

▶ **Accommodations:** The Exploration Foundation recommends Hotel Nuevo Boston (+504 2237-9411) for your pre- and post-trip overnights in Tegucigalpa.

18

DESTINATION

HORNSTRANDIR (AND BEYOND)

RECOMMENDED BY **Rúnar Karlsson**

Whether you believe that the fjords of the Westfjords region of Iceland were carved by trolls or formed by retreating glaciers, few would argue that the seat of a kayak is a great place from which to take them in. A kayak can also help you uncover the treasures of the Hornstrandir Nature Reserve. "People like to kayak around the Hornstrandir because there are so few people here," Rúnar Karlsson said. "Nature rules—you're in a wilderness. There's abundant birdlife—the spectacle of the seabirds at Hælavík and Hornvík is a wonder of nature. There's a good chance you'll find porpoises on the water, and if you're fortunate, humpback whales. Another appeal is that in the late spring and summer, we have twenty-four hours of light. Some days, we might not start paddling until the afternoon, and we can go until two A.M."

Iceland is nothing if not dramatic, a land of fire and ice, of stark, treeless landscapes and a rich mythical folklore that's quite alive among Icelanders. The fire comes from the island's pronounced geothermal activities, which provide a considerable amount of heat and hot water for Iceland's more than three hundred thousand residents, and from the island's over two dozen active volcanoes. The ice comes from glaciers, which have carved many fjords along Iceland's three-thousand-mile coastline, and constitute 11 percent of the nation's landmass. Much of Iceland was formed (and is forming) from volcanic flows, which explains some of its rugged topography. Most of the population lives on or near the coastline, which is warmed by the North Atlantic Drift Current, making it far more habitable than Greenland, 180 miles to the west.

The Hornstrandir sits at the top of the Westfjords, the northwesternmost region of Iceland. The coastline is steep and carved by many fjords. Once, this majestic but unforgiving land was populated by hearty souls who eked out a living fishing, collecting bird eggs

OPPOSITE:
Kayakers visiting the Hornstrandir Nature Reserve will encounter many seabirds, perhaps a few whales, and few if any other people.

DESTINATION

19

from the region's bird cliffs, and raising livestock. By the middle of the twentieth century, however, the travails of making a living—and the disconnectedness from the rest of Iceland—had driven all the human occupants away. "In some places, as you paddle along, you see the remnants of old houses," Rúnar continued. "You can't help but marvel at what a hard life the inhabitants must have had and how they managed to survive." While there are no people living in the Hornstrandir now, there are many Arctic foxes. The only land mammal native to Iceland, the foxes are a great attraction to the region.

Rúnar has paddled extensively in the Hornstrandir and the other waters of the Westfjords region. He described a few highlights visiting kayakers can anticipate. "My favorite fjord to visit is Lonafjordur. The head of the fjord is very narrow, but once you're inside, it feels like you're in a lagoon. ('Lona' means lagoon.) It's surrounded by steep cliffs with snowfields, and there are crystal clear rivers flowing in. It's very calm in this fjord, and there's a nice campsite. There's even a little hot spring there, though you have to time your visits right, as it's submerged at high tide. Another fjord that's fun to visit is Leirufjordur (or Silt Fjord). There's a clear line of demarcation between the clear water and muddied water, which is off-color from silt coming in from the Drangajökull Glacier. On some trips, we'll head into the Bay of Ísafjarðardjúp. Here, you have the best chance of finding humpback whales. You can hear them spouting in the distance. Once you figure out which direction they're coming from, you head that way. You often can reach them.

"One of the most dramatic paddles in the Westfjords takes you to Hornvík Bay, in the northern part of the reserve. This is the site of one of Iceland's great bird cliffs, Hornbjarg. The cliff rises almost two thousand feet from the sea. At times, over six million seabirds nest here—guillemots, razorbills, eiders, puffins, kittiwakes, and fulmars. There are guillemots diving for food and occasionally falling rocks, so we don't get too close. The breathtaking sight is rivaled by the sound. It's truly a one-of-a-kind experience. I find it difficult to imagine how men would scale these same cliffs with hemp ropes to gather eggs for food."

You won't have to gather eggs from Hornbjarg to make your meals, though paddlers around the Hornstrandir can gather their sustenance if they so choose . . . and if they know where to look. "There are many edible plants and spices we can gather, as well as mussels," Rúnar added. "We can catch char and trout, too. But we also bring along lamb, which we'll barbecue." (No hákarl, Iceland's infamous fermented shark, is served.)

Rúnar recalled an evening that seems to define the Hornstrandir paddling experience. "I was out with a group of Americans who were strong paddlers. I could see that the wind was changing, and I suggested that we combine two days of travel into one so we could get ahead of the wind. We completed what would normally be a full day's paddle and pulled in at the site of an abandoned house and had dinner. Then we continued into the evening to cover what would have been the next day's distance. It was the summer solstice, and still calm. At one point we came around the cliffs at the edge of a fjord and suddenly, there was the sun setting into the sea. Everything was glowing red, with hundreds of seabirds flying about. As we continued another few kilometers to our camping spot for the night, the sun began rising again."

RÚNAR KARLSSON holds a degree in geography and has worked as a mountaineering and mountain biking guide. He also worked as a tourism consultant for a few years but felt it was time to put his skills into practice and put up an adventure operation, Borea Adventures, with other good people. Skiing, ice and rock climbing, sea kayaking, and sailing are his favorite sports and now part of his job. He has scaled six-thousand-meter peaks in Peru, led skiing and kayaking expeditions in Greenland, climbed in the Alps, and paraglided in the Pyrenees. Rúnar gained much of his training from years of volunteering for mountain rescue teams in Iceland and has especially trained for avalanche search-and-rescue and wilderness first aid.

If You Go

▶ **Getting There:** Trips generally stage in Ísafjörður, which is served from Reykjavík by Air Iceland (+354 570 3030; www.airiceland.is).

▶ **Best Time to Visit:** Mid-May through August.

▶ **Guides/Outfitters:** Borea Adventures (+354 456 3322; www.boreaadventures.com) leads a number of different trips in the West Fjords. Wild West Fjords (www.wildwest fjords.com) also orchestrates paddling tours.

▶ **Level of Difficulty:** Wind can often be avoided, but paddlers should have a moderate level of experience.

▶ **Accommodations:** The Westfjords Tourist Information Center (+354-450-8060; www .westfjords.is) lists lodging options in greater Ísafjörður.

DESTINATION 19

MIDDLE FORK OF THE SALMON

RECOMMENDED BY **Al Bukowsky**

Paddlers love it for its more than three hundred rapids. Fly anglers love it for its freely rising cutthroat trout. And infrequent outdoors people—including presidents and other assorted potentates—embrace it as a place where they can comfortably immerse themselves in one of the last great wilderness areas left in the lower forty-eight.

The Middle Fork has flowed through Al Bukowsky's adult life as much as the blood in his veins. "I started working on the Rogue River as a boy in the late fifties," Al began. "Though we were on a pretty famous river, the trips that always came up in conversation among the guides were the Grand Canyon and the Middle Fork. A couple of Oregonians— Buzz Hatch and Woody Hindman—began running the Middle Fork in the forties in McKenzie drift boats, and word got back to Oregon about the wonders of the river. [Hindman helped design the drift boat that's so popular with anglers on western waters.] I started running it in 1978 and have probably been down the river 350 times. It's always inspiring, in many different ways. First, there's the canyon's spectacular beauty. It changes significantly as you lose elevation—you begin in alpine terrain and end in canyon country [the float begins at an elevation of seven thousand feet and finishes at less than four thousand feet]. When people first see the Sawtooths, their mouths drop open—it's like the Tetons with foothills. Then there's the incredibly clear water. Anglers love it, as you can see the trout come up from the river bottom to take dry flies. Another special facet of the Middle Fork are the camps. Though it's a wilderness river, all the campsites are assigned to boaters ahead of time. Most are on benches above the river and have great vistas. Yet you're secluded enough that you'd never know anyone else was around. Finally, there are great hikes along most of the river. A trail follows it for seventy miles, so you can take off and go for a hike to see Native American pictographs and pioneer homesteads or soak in hidden hot springs."

OPPOSITE:
A party negotiates
the tight rapids
of the upper
section of the
Middle Fork.

The Middle Fork carves its way 106 miles through the second-largest wilderness area in the United States—the 2.4 million-acre Frank Church–River of No Return Wilderness—in the heart of central Idaho. (Efforts to preserve the area—including the Wilderness Act of 1964 and the Wild and Scenic Rivers Act—were championed by Idaho senator Frank Church.) Rafters generally stage in the town of Stanley, are shuttled to the put-in at Boundary Creek, and then float the river over the course of six days and five nights to the take-out below the Middle Fork's confluence with the main stem of the Salmon River. In its upper reaches, the Middle Fork is an intimate, high-gradient stream, hemmed in closely by thick forests of Douglas fir and spruce. As you proceed downriver, the canyon opens up to expose jaw-dropping crags of Idaho batholith that climb to the sky. The area is home to elk, deer, moose, mountain lion, and black bear, though these critters are seldom encountered, as they summer higher in the mountains. Bighorn sheep and mountain goats, however, are often seen cavorting on the cliffsides. Several natural hot springs present themselves along the river; Sunflower, a hot spring that includes natural pools and a makeshift shower, is especially nurturing for sore paddling or casting shoulders.

"Each time you run the Middle Fork, it's a different experience from a paddling perspective," Al continued. "The levels are always changing, and different rapids run much differently at different water levels. At the beginning of the season when there's a good runoff from the snowmelt, the first fifteen or twenty miles are especially fast. There are no eddies where you can pull off, and the water is up in the brush; it's like you're being flushed down the river. In late summer, you find yourself picking your way through lots of rock gardens. My favorite water level is a little bit above medium. That's when the well-known rapids—Velvet Falls, Pistol Creek, Tappan Falls, Haystack, Hell's Half Mile, Powerhouse, Weber, and Rubber, among them—run the best. Pistol Creek (a Class IV) can be really gnarly at certain levels; Rubber, though it's a Class III, has huge waves and is one of the most powerful spots on the river."

Al runs the Middle Fork in two different crafts: paddle rafts, where guests provide manpower and a guide steers, and drift boats, which can accommodate two anglers. "Rowing a drift boat with two anglers on the Middle Fork is about as challenging as it gets for an oarsman," Al added. "The difference between rowing a drift boat and a raft is huge. You can't go much higher as far as technical rapids are concerned. If you can row a drift boat down the Middle Fork, you're at the top of your game." (The Middle Fork is one of the great strongholds of the westslope cutthroat trout, one of the Rocky's endemic trout species, first discovered by Lewis and Clark. Even if you're not on a fishing-specific trip, throw a fly rod in with your gear, as there's generally fishing available at each camp.)

Meals are a big part of any extended river trip, and Al takes great pride in the meals his team provides—Pacific salmon, grilled chicken, and, in Al's words, "one of the best pork chops you'll ever have." He and one of his guides, Mike Gehrman, shared a favorite story concerning said pork chops. "We have a fairly close relationship with the staff at the Flying B Ranch, which is at river mile 67. We stop every trip, so we know the folks who work there. A few years ago we had some kids on our trip, so we invited the horse wranglers at the B to come to dinner at Sheep Creek camp. This way the kids would get to see real horses and cowboys. Well the Flying B guys dressed the part and everyone was pleased with the show. It was pork chop night. We served a double-cut two-inch-thick pork chop cooked on mountain mahogany coals. It's a full meal with salad and topped off with a Dutch-oven apple crisp for dessert.

"Well, the kids on the trip couldn't eat a whole pork chop so there were some extras. Near the end of the meal I asked if anyone wanted an extra pork chop. One of the wranglers was a skinny kid, about 145 pounds. He said he'd take one. He'd already finished his own. Well he finished the second one, and there were still a couple of more pork chops left. No one was taking them, so he mentioned that if nobody wanted them he wouldn't mind having another. Then it was dessert time. This same wrangler had one apple crisp and then another. One of the guests was astonished. She said, 'My God, how can you eat that much.' The wrangler slowly turned and said, 'There were seven kids in our family, and you learned early—you gotta take the pie while the pie was being passed or you might not get any.'

"I've always remembered his wisdom. There are times in life when you need to do something or you won't get another chance. The line 'you gotta take the pie while the pie was being passed' is some good philosophy to hang on to."

AL BUKOWSKY is a native Oregonian who was introduced to fishing and boating on the Rogue River in the 1950s by his uncles and mother. Al—along with his wife, Jeana—formed Solitude River Trips in 1976 on the Rogue. He began guiding on the Middle Fork of the Salmon in 1978 and a few years later purchased the rafting company from Mel Norrick. Al knows the river like the back of his hand and can spin tales for hours about its amazing history.

► **Getting There:** Most rafters fly into Boise; from here it's a three-hour drive to Stanley or a short flight. McCall Aviation (800-992-6559; www.mccallaviation.com) provides air taxi service to Stanley and Salmon (near the take-out).

► **Best Time to Visit:** Most float the Middle Fork from June through September; water can be high and fast in the early spring and a little "skinny" in late summer.

► **Guides/Outfitters:** A number of outfitters lead trips on the Middle Fork, including Solitude River Trips (800-396-1776; www.rivertrips.com). A very limited number of permits for private trips are available each summer.

► **Level of Experience:** Those floating with guides need no prior paddling experience. Self-guided paddlers should have extensive Class IV+ experience.

► **Accommodations:** Al recommends Mountain Village Resort (800-843-5475; www .mountainvillage.com) for lodging in Stanley before trips launch.

20

DESTINATION

OWYHEE RIVER

RECOMMENDED BY **Peter Grubb**

The Owyhee may be the best western desert river you've never heard of.

"I have a love affair with the Owyhee for a number of reasons," began Peter Grubb. "I grew up in a desert region in central California and have an affinity for desert ecosystems. The Owyhee is in the northern reaches of the Great Basin, squarely in sagebrush country, with its special fragrance and profusion of wildflowers in the spring. The desert here has subtle life. There's plenty of flora and fauna—amazing birds and reptiles—but it's not in your face. Running the Owyhee has a number of logistical challenges. There's a limited time when you can run it, and even then, there has to be just the right amount of water. It's a pretty finite number of paddlers that run the Owyhee, especially the upper sections. For this reason, you can't take it for granted, and that makes it more special."

The Owyhee rises in northeastern Nevada, above the town of Elko, and flows over two hundred miles in a generally northwesterly direction to its terminus with the Snake. En route, it passes across a portion of southwestern Idaho in Owyhee County and has its longest stretch in Malheur County, Oregon. (It takes its name, incidentally, from three trappers of Hawaiian descent who were sent to set traps on a then-unnamed river in 1819. They were believed to have been killed by Native Americans; the river they were sent to explore was named in their honor, "Owyhee" being a phonetic spelling of Hawaii.) The Owyhee is not a huge river, yet it cuts through dramatic canyonland country. In some places, walls of rhyolite climb nearly a thousand feet from the water; in others, you paddle through formations that resemble oversize sand castles. The multicolored canyons bring to mind the national parks of Bryce Canyon and Zion.

When it comes to paddling the Owyhee, there are four discrete options available, each with its own charms and challenges. The first segment that can be run is the Lower

Owyhee, which stretches the last fifty miles above Lake Owyhee, in Oregon. While the canyons may be slightly less dramatic than on the upper sections of the river, the rapids are more moderate. "This section is most approachable," Peter continued. "We generally do it at a leisurely pace, five days/four nights or six days/five nights. There's plenty of time for hikes to view Native American pictographs and for bird-watching. This float appeals to a wide audience." Stepping up the intensity level is the Middle Owyhee. This thirty-eight-mile stretch begins at Three Forks (where the main stem Owyhee and the North and South Forks meet) and ends near the town of Rome. The middle segment has a number of Class IV rapids and one Class V, fittingly called Widowmaker. It is likely the most challenging rapid on the entire system, with a steep gradient and huge holes and boulders that create exceedingly tight lines. "We opt to line our rafts through Widowmaker," Peter said. "You're so far out in the wilderness, it's just not worth the chance of a mishap."

For seasoned rafters and kayakers—and those with a flair for adventure—the upper sections of the Owyhee hold the most appeal. Among aficionados, the East and South Fork are among the most sought-after floats in North America. Each is approximately 120 miles and flows through some of the most remote country in the west. And both require some special considerations. "The upper sections of the Owyhee are for the highest echelon of paddler, people who have done all the big-name rivers and are looking for new frontiers. To do this trip, you have to be quite physically fit, agile, and flexible. I run these trips in expedition-style—which is to say that we use smaller rafts and/or inflatable kayaks, more guides (a one-to-two guide-to-guest ratio), and have fewer amenities. We need to travel lighter in part because of the technical nature of some of the rapids, and in part because each section requires at least one portage, sometimes two."

The East Fork launches near the Duck Valley Indian Reservation on the Nevada-Idaho border and is the more technical of the two floats, with many tight, almost impassable rapids. The South Fork is a bit mellower for the first three days; on the latter half of the trip, it merges with the East Fork, and you follow the same course. Thanks to its extreme isolation and the fact that very few humans make their way down the canyon each year, the East and South Forks afford the best opportunity of spying the region's wildlife—avifauna like golden eagles, peregrine falcons, and many different hawks; mammals including beaver, otter, pronghorn antelope, and desert bighorn sheep; and reptiles like collared lizards, horned toads, rattlesnakes, and western racers.

OPPOSITE:
Very few paddlers
get to experience
the wonders of
the Owyhee's
dramatic canyons
during its brief
spring rafting
season.

DESTINATION **21**

"Running the East or South Forks of the Owyhee is a holistic experience for me," Peter opined. "There's some challenging white water, but it's really about being dwarfed by the beauty of the place—like a section on the East Fork called the Tules. You float through this ancient valley with towering cliffs on a very calm section of water. There are cattails growing up along the banks (hence the name), and often, the calls of raptors ringing across the canyon. When you're here, you feel like you're the only person on earth, and that the world is all right. It's no different than it's been for a thousand years, and no one has screwed it up.

"Overall, the remoteness gives your adventure a sense of urgency, of being on the edge. You're on your own, there's not another group coming behind you."

PETER GRUBB founded ROW Adventures back in 1979, after discovering river running on the East Coast. Certified by the National Association for Interpretation as a certified interpretation guide, Peter also completed certification in 2004 to train other guides in the art of cultural and natural history interpretation. He also speaks French and plays the guitar. ROW's administrative duties keep Peter in the office much of the time, but his heart is still on the river. He lives with his wife, Betsy Bowen, in Coeur d'Alene. His travels have taken him to over twenty U.S. states and some thirty-five countries.

21

DESTINATION

If You Go

▶ **Getting There:** Most visitors will assemble in Boise, Idaho. From Boise, you'll be transferred to the appropriate put-in, anywhere from two to four hours' distance.

▶ **Best Time to Visit:** The Owyhee can be run with rafts from early April through June. Seasoned kayakers can run the upper sections of the river through July.

▶ **Guides/Outfitters:** ROW Adventures (800-451-6034; www.rowadventures.com) leads trips on all four segments of the Owyhee.

▶ **Level of Difficulty:** The Lower Owyhee is suitable for less seasoned paddlers. The other sections are recommended for highly experienced rafters/kayakers.

▶ **Accommodations:** The Boise Convention and Visitors Bureau (www.boise.org) lists lodging options for the night before your trip begins.

KOMODO ISLANDS

RECOMMENDED BY **Peter Miller**

If the Komodo Islands were to launch an advertising campaign for kayakers, it might be:
"Come for the dragons, stay for the snorkeling."

"I've tried to put my finger on what makes the Komodos so special, and it's hard to do," Peter Miller began. "In Australia, we talk about the vibe of a place, the positive energy that comes at you. The Komodos have that vibe. Your plane lands in Flores, and you might still be a bit stressed. Within a few hours, the worries are being washed away. You're able to immerse yourself in a kaleidoscope of colors and movement—the rugged hills, the turquoise waters, and the plethora of marine life below the surface."

The region of Komodo encompasses a string of volcanic islands in eastern Indonesia, resting between the larger landmasses of Sumbawa and Flores, roughly 230 miles east of Bali. Most of the area is contained in Komodo National Park, a seven-hundred-square-mile protected area that includes roughly two dozen islands, including the larger islands—Rinca, Gili Mota, Nusa Kode, and Padar. The park was established in 1980, largely to protect dwindling populations of the world's largest lizards—its namesake, the Komodo dragon—and was listed as a UNESCO World Heritage Site in recognition of its unique animal life above and below the surface of the surrounding Flores Sea. Like the Lombok Strait to the west, the Komodo region serves as a funnel between the Indian and Pacific Oceans. The flow of water and accompanying nutrients make for a rich stew that sustains robust sea life, including over 250 species of coral, 1,000 species of fish, and marine mammals ranging from passing blue whales to dugongs, a member of the manatee family that lives solely in salt water. There's also a seemingly endless array of remote beaches—some with pink sand, some with gray, others with black—that see few if any other biped visitors.

Peter's exploration of the Komodos unfolds over five days. The proximity of the islands in the archipelago allows kayakers to paddle from one island to the next, camping on pristine beaches on uninhabited islands along the way. "We use a modified boat called a Komodo Kayak," Peter explained. "They were originally developed in Tasmania. They're a little wider than conventional boats, hence very stable, and available as singles or doubles. I've never seen one flip. The waters can get a bit choppy, as both the Indian and Pacific Oceans ebb through the region, creating a rush of water through the islands. Sometimes the flow can create modest whirlpools. You can see them swirling around, and you can even nose in and get a ride. It can get windy at times, but we always have a support boat nearby in case anyone gets tired.

"I like to wake up with the sunrise. It's already nearly 80°F at dawn, and the water is warm; you can dive in first thing, and there's no shock. Once we have breakfast and break camp, we start on our way with a leisurely pace. The snorkeling and diving around the Komodos are some of the best in the world, especially for seeing soft corals. If we pass a reef that looks enticing, we jump out of the boats to do some snorkeling. You don't see tons of fish, but the soft coral gardens are like a Garden of Eden underwater." Immense purple gorgonian fans are a highlight. Though reef fish are not present in great numbers, sea turtles, manta rays, and spinner dolphins are frequently encountered.

(Note: Stand-up paddling adventures around the Komodos—which offer an ongoing perspective of the underwater pageantry—are also offered.)

No visitors to the Komodo Islands will want to leave before meeting the region's most famous inhabitant, the Komodo dragon. Komodo dragons average nearly eight feet in length and weigh between 120 and 150 pounds; the largest recorded specimen reached nearly ten feet in length and 366 pounds. The dragons feed primarily on the island's small Timor deer but have been known to eat eggs (of other dragons and turtles), buffalo, boar, wild horses, and monkeys. (The venom that's secreted from between their teeth is very powerful and enables the lizards to take down large prey. If the venom doesn't do its deadly work, bacteria in the dragon's mouth will lead to infections. These are usually fatal.) Dragon numbers have been impacted by declining populations of deer, though the current population is holding steady at roughly three thousand.

"Because we're paddling, we can get to the ranger station at Komodo Island ahead of the tourist boats," Peter explained. [Camping on the island is prohibited.] "We're usually there by seven; the dragons are quite active at this time. We do a walking tour on trails

22

DESTINATION

through their habitat, where we usually come upon water buffalo and gray macaque monkeys. I've witnessed the lizards with their kills. There might be several dragons around the carcass, squabbling over it like lions. The dominant male gets the best bits. They are very prehistoric creatures and fit in well with the prehistoric setting."

Though the dragons provoke strong impressions, Peter's most lasting Komodo memories concern sea creatures. "Sometimes when you're snorkeling, you almost forget you're underwater," he recalled. "You forget that you have to breathe, but you're body isn't struggling—you're so lost in the moment. Once I was in such a state and had dove down to look closer at a reef. Suddenly it became dark. I turned to look up, and there was a group of manta rays sailing by above me in slow motion. It took my breath away, even though I didn't have much breath left!"

PETER MILLER has always been the sort of person who says, "I wonder what is over there?" "On land, that can be a little problematic as I often find myself cutting through jungles or scrambling up rocks. But on the sea, I have total freedom." This wanderlust has led Peter to open new areas to sea kayaking, pioneering paddles in the Komodo Islands in Indonesia and the Tigak Sea in Papua New Guinea.

If You Go

▶ **Getting There:** Trips begin and end on Flores. To reach Flores, fly to Densapar, Bali, which is served from Los Angeles by a number of carriers. From Densapar, you'll fly to Labuhan Bajo, which is served by TransNusa (+62 380 822 555; www.transnusa.co.id).

▶ **Best Time to Visit:** March to December; January and February bring monsoons.

▶ **Guides/Outfitters:** No Roads Expeditions (+61 3 9598 8581; www.noroads.com.au) leads a number of different kayaking trips around the Komodos.

▶ **Level of Difficulty:** No previous paddling experience is necessary, though visitors should be in decent physical condition.

▶ **Accommodations:** Guests generally stay at the Bajo Komodo Ecolodge (+62 361 74 74 205; bajoecolodge.com) on the day before the expedition begins.

ELBA

RECOMMENDED BY **Barbara Kossy**

"I like to describe a paddling vacation on the island of Elba as civilized kayaking," Barbara Kossy began. "The island is rugged, with lots of topographic variety. The water is clear, warm, and, except for winter, very calm, as there's little tidal influence. There are lots of options in terms of stopping points along the coastline. You can push yourself hard or linger at the beach . . . and if you choose the latter, some of the beaches have fine little restaurants. When the day is done, wonderful Ligurian and Florentine meals await you— both seafood salads and the Tuscan food of the woods. Given the island's rich history, a trip here can also be described as kayaking through civilization."

The island of Elba rests twelve miles off the coast of Tuscany in the Tyrrhenian Sea; it's the largest of the islands that make up the Tuscan Archipelago. Some may recall Elba as the site of Napoleon Bonparte's first exile, though the ancient Etruscans and Romans knew the island as a rich source of iron. The former mines are now part of a national park. Elba is now primarily a vacation retreat. "You see many Germans and Scandinavians vacationing on Elba," Barbara added, "as well as the Italian middle class. There's a great vacation infrastructure there in terms of villas for rent and a constant flow of summer festivals."

Elba—and for that matter, Italy—is a relatively new paddling destination. Barbara explained her discovery. "I started kayaking around San Francisco in 1989," she continued, "and soon became interested in kayaking travel. Baja California and Alaska were the places that came up in conversation with other paddlers. Around the same time, I took a trip to Italy. In the Cinque Terre, there were a few little kayaks around—modified riverboats, not expedition-style sea kayaks. My interest was piqued. In the back of *Sea Kayaker* magazine, I came upon a little ad from the Italian Sea Kayaking Association. I wrote to

OPPOSITE:
As you make
your way along
the coast, Elba
boasts more
than one hundred
named beaches—
some with
excellent cafes.

23

DESTINATION

the address in English and said I'd love to come kayaking in Italy, did they have any suggestions? I also offered to take any interested parties out on the water in California. Pretty soon I received a letter back in English, inviting me to visit the group's kayaking center in Elba. I went and met Gaudenzio Coltelli—one of the progenitors of Italian sea kayaking. Gaudenzio is an exceptional teacher and guide and knows Elba extremely well.

"I enjoyed my first visit to Elba a great deal and told Gaudenzio as much. It was during that visit that he and his peers at the Italian Sea Kayaking Association asked me if I could help them bring other Americans to Elba to kayak. I ended up helping them develop a tour." The itinerary Barbara and Gaudenzio designed uses the village of Marciana Marina on the island's north shore as a base for day trips. "The village has a nice little square, great restaurants, a nice marina, and artisans on the streets," she said. "It's also very accessible—just an hour south of Pisa by ferry." From Marciana Marina, paddlers can head east or west. "When you head east, you start out in a protected natural harbor," Barbara continued, "in the shadow of a Pisan watchtower that dates back to the twelfth century. Pirates used to terrorize ships in the area, but the Pisans had the military power to suppress them. You head out past the fishing boats in the harbor and along a steep, rocky shore that's dotted with vacation villas. I might stop at Isola Paolina, an island just offshore. It's named for Napoleon's sister; the story goes that she'd sunbathe nude on the island. From Isola Paolina I continue east to the town of Procchio, where there are several pleasant beaches and coves. (Overall, Elba has over a hundred named beaches.) In one little cove, you can view remnants of Nazi bunkers, as the Germans occupied Elba during World War II. You can't help juxtapose the twelfth-century towers back in Marciana Marina with the more recent fortifications. At Proccio Beach, there's a little café where you can get a great pasta salad, as well as gelato. It's a nice surprise to find this nice lunch spot on an isolated beach. [Gaudenzio also offers circumnavigations of Elba. Guests camp on deserted beaches and visit towns for supplies and meals. The trip takes about five days.]

"I should add that Elba provides a very benign environment to paddle in. There's a road along the perimeter of the island, and there are lots of fishermen around. It's easy to come up with a backup plan. If it happens to be windy on the north side of the island, it's not a problem to load up the boats and drive to the south side. And if it's rainy or just too windy to go out on the water, there are great hiking trails in the middle of the island, as well as interesting little museums. If you're with Gaudenzio, you're in good hands, as it seems he knows everyone on the island."

DESTINATION **23**

If you paddle west out of Marciana Marina, the coastline is a bit less populated, and the water is so clear that you can see fish swimming from inside your boat. "I recall paddling back to Marciana early one evening after a trip to the west," Barbara said. "The sun was setting behind me, and the twilight over the town and the craggy shoreline was spectacular. As I made my way into the harbor, the lights of the Marciana were beginning to come on, but there was still the twilight glow, silhouetting palm trees against the seaside architecture, with Monte Capanne [Elba's tallest point at 3,340 feet] in the background."

BARBARA KOSSY has been traveling to Italy since 1983 and sea kayaking since 1989. In 1996, she combined these passions by organizing trips for Sea Kayak Italy. Since that time, she has organized kayaking trips on the islands of Elba, Sicily, Sardinia, and on Bulgaria's Black Sea. Born in Chicago, Barbara attended Antioch College in Ohio and the Art Institute of Chicago. She lives near Half Moon Bay, California, and is an active environmentalist, serving on the board of the San Mateo County Resource Conservation District.

If You Go

▶ **Getting There:** Visitors can fly into Pisa or Florence, transfer to Piombino and take a ferry to Portoferraio on Moby Lines (+49 (0)611 14020; www.mobylines.com). You can also reach Elba by air from a number of European cities on InterSky (www.flyintersky .com) and SkyWork (+43 5574 48800 46; www.flyskywork.com).

▶ **Best Time to Visit:** The climate is hospitable to paddling from mid-spring through mid-fall.

▶ **Guides/Outfitters:** Sea Kayak Italy (www.seakayakitaly.it), Gaudenzio Coltelli's company, is the paddler's main option on Elba. Barbara Kossy (650-728-8720; www.barbara kossy.com) handles bookings in North America.

▶ **Level of Difficulty:** Paddling around Elba does not require previous experience.

▶ **Accommodations:** A host of lodging options around Marciana Marina are listed on Sea Kayak Italy (www.seakayakitaly.it).

MEKONG RIVER

RECOMMENDED BY **Brad Ludden**

The Mekong is one of the world's longest rivers. Beginning in the Three Rivers Nature Reserve on the Tibetan Plateau, it flows some 2,700 miles in a southerly direction, touching Burma, Thailand, Laos, Cambodia, and Vietnam before reaching the Mekong Delta and the South China Sea. Both a major trade route and a source of sustenance for millions of people along its banks (the Mekong supports over 1,300 species of fish), it's a river many picture as wide and placid—an image no doubt fostered by representations of the delta in popular media. While this characterization is true of much of the Mekong's course, there's a section of the river along the border between Cambodia and Laos that is emerging as one of the world's most unique and challenging kayaking spots: Si Phan Don (the Four Thousand Islands).

"The Four Thousand Islands region of the Mekong is easily the most captivating water I've ever paddled," professional kayaker Brad Ludden began. "It's unlike anywhere I've ever been—the character of the river, the people, and the history of the place. There aren't any crocodiles, no civil wars, and you won't be taken hostage. From both a paddling and travel perspective, it's an amazing combination."

The Four Thousand Islands region is in the Champasak Province of southern Laos. Here, thanks to a fault line along the riverbed, the river braids to a width of more than eight miles, with Laos on river left, Cambodia, river right. The geologic anomaly has created thousands of islands, many of which are submerged during times of high water. It's also created an abundance of waterfalls and rapids. "The thing that's very odd," Brad continued, "is that you encounter the white water as you move left to right in the river, not as you move downstream. Instead of constantly moving downriver to find new water, you can stay on one island and paddle left or right to find new water . . . or hire a boat to drop

OPPOSITE:
In higher water conditions, paddlers in the Four Thousand Islands region will navigate flora as well as tricky rapids.

DESTINATION 24

113

you off and pick you up at nearby islands. The mode of transport is long dugout canoes with long prop motors. The driveshaft alone is ten feet long."

Reaching the Four Thousand Islands poses a challenge on par with some of its Class V and VI rapids. After touching down in Bangkok, you'll take an overnight train (or plane) east to near the border with Laos. Then you get on a rickety truck, somehow secure your kayak, and head to the border. After you've cleared the border, you get on another truck that takes you to the Laotian side of the river. From here, someone with one of the afore-mentioned dugout canoes will take you to one of the islands—usually Don Khon and Don Khong. "We found a lady on Don Khon who runs a little guesthouse," Brad said. "We stayed in a bamboo hut at the top of the island. It was back in 2000, but she charged about a quarter a night. She also cooks wonderful meals. Laotian food is similar to Thai, though milder. If you want to eat fish, her husband will go out and catch one. I've visited some out-of-the-way places where I simply couldn't eat the food. If you're a traveler with an uneasy stomach, you'll be fine on Don Khon. Between the food, the water, the hospital-ity, and the low prices, it was the only time I felt rich as a kayaker."

From a kayaking perspective, Four Thousand Islands offers something for white-water enthusiasts of varying levels. "You can find plenty of chutes that are Class I or Class II, and you can find unrunnable Class VIIs—and everything in between," Brad explained. "There's something for everyone. For a skilled kayaker, every day is like Christmas—there's something new waiting, as there are literally thousands of channels to run. There's one peculiar hazard you need to look out for—fish hooks. The villagers fish by hanging lines across the channels, which are carved canyons, and they hang hooks off the bottom. As the water drops, they string another line with new hooks. Ultimately, you might have a spiderweb of lines hanging across the channels, and you have to be aware of them.

"Many of the channels have nice sandy beaches adjacent to them. It's like a fusion of the beach and kayaking lifestyles. At the end of the day, you've usually made your way to the bottom of the island. You can find someone to help you haul your boat back up to the guesthouse. In the pools below some of the rapids, you might find freshwater [Irrawaddy] dolphins. If you stick your paddle in the water and put your ear to the other end, you can hear them."

Brad found the paddling amazing but was even more blown away by the villagers. "The Laotian people are so calm and laid-back. Laos was the most heavily bombed coun-try in history, even though it was a neutral party in the Vietnam War. [More than 2.5 million tons of cluster bombs rained down on Laos from 1964 to 1973, courtesy of the United States; some 75 million bombs failed to detonate, and each year since, an average of three hundred Lao people have been injured or killed by stepping on bombs.] Despite this, the people are the warmest and most welcoming—and most forgiving—that I've encountered in all my travels."

People in less developed countries with less time and resources for leisure may wonder at the recreational pastimes some Westerners pursue. *Why fish with fur and feathers when nets work so well? Why climb that mountain when there's nothing to eat up there?* The Laotians on Don Khong may have had their doubts about Brad's kayaking endeavors, but instead of dismissing them, they came to his aid in a uniquely Laotian way. "There was a particularly difficult rapid that I'd been trying to run," he recalled. "I'd lost equipment in the waterfall portion and had even broken a boat. Eventually I learned that the local people believe that Buddha lives behind the waterfall. Somehow I was messing with karma. Once the woman we'd been staying with understood that I wanted to paddle through the rapid, she told one of my friends that we needed to have a *baci* performed. A Baci [an animist ritual quite prevalent in Laos and parts of Thailand] is basically a ritual to call back an individual's protective spirits [or *kwan*], who may have wandered off to return and assist the individual in a time of need or for a special occasion. Our hostess arranged everything. The village elder conducted a ceremony to make the case for why my spirits needed to come back and help me. Many of the other villagers were present. At the conclusion, he tied white thread around my right wrist. [The thread is symbolic of peace, harmony, good fortune, good health, and human warmth and community.]

"After the Baci, I ran the rapid perfectly, as the villagers cheered. As we celebrated, we watched the Irrawaddy dolphins feeding as the sun set. The feeling of success was exhilarating, but the sense of being accepted into the villagers' culture and being so supported was even more inspiring."

BRAD LUDDEN received his first kayak when he was nine, and at age twelve he was traveling and competing internationally. By eighteen, he had kayaked in over twenty countries and found his true passion within the sport, first descents. Through his first descents he found immense challenge, adventure, community, and personal growth. At age twelve, cancer went from being just some random word to something very personal, when his aunt was diagnosed with breast cancer at the age of thirty-eight. After watching her endure cancer and seeing how little support there was available to her, Brad started volunteering for a local pediatric oncology program by teaching the participants how to kayak. At eighteen, he started working on an organization that would soon become First Descents. Its goal is to help young adults by giving them the life-changing experience of kayaking. "I wanted to re-create the experience of a first descent, which had so greatly impacted my life, for people like my aunt who really needed it," Brad said. "Even though thousands of people have been down the rivers they're kayaking, at camp it's still the first time they've been down it, and that's the magic of First Descents." Brad continues to kayak professionally for Teva, Dagger, Adventure Technology Paddles, Kokatat, and Smith Optics and still pursues his own adventures on rivers around the world in addition to his work at First Descents.

If You Go

▶ **Getting There:** You can reach Laos by bus or train from Bangkok, though it's easiest to fly to Pakse, Laos, which is served by Lao Airlines (www.laoairlines.com). From here, it's a two-hour private mini-bus ride to the village of Nakasang, and then a short longtail boat ride to the islands.

▶ **Best Time to Visit:** November to March has the coolest weather. Visitors generally want to avoid the rainy season, which runs from May to October.

▶ **Guides/Outfitters:** This is not a trip that most people will want to tackle on their own, given the on-the-ground logistics and language barriers. Mick O'Shea at Wildside Asia Travel (+66 813601905; mickomail@yahoo.com) and Steve Van Beek (+66 2 653 9712; www.stevevanbeek.com) both have experience helping kayakers visit the Four Thousand Islands, including transportation and lodging.

▶ **Level of Difficulty:** While there are Class I and II runs here, many rapids are extremely challenging, and the overall adventure is not for the casual traveler.

GREATER DAMARISCOTTA RIVER

RECOMMENDED BY **Tom Armstrong**

As the crow or puffin flies, the coast of Maine stretches 250 miles from Kittery to Calais. But if you were to stretch a string from the Piscataqua River in the south to the northern edge of Passamaquoddy Bay and follow every inch of shoreline, it would extend over 3,500 miles. The number of bays, harbors, estuaries, and coves—a seemingly inexhaustible number of places to tuck in and explore—make the Pine Tree State a paddler's paradise. The appeals are unending. Casco Bay in the south showcases the thriving waterfront of Maine's largest city, Portland; Southwest Harbor and Acadia National Park to the northeast embody the state's famously rugged coast. For Tom Armstrong, Maine's many kayaking possibilities come together around the Damariscotta River. "You have a great river and countless coves that you can explore, plus some challenging offshore water for more seasoned paddlers," he said. "You'll see seals, sea birds, possibly porpoise, beautiful rocky coast, schooners out of Boothbay Harbor, and much of the fauna that calls the coast home."

The town of Damariscotta is near the beginning of what's commonly referred to as "midcoast" Maine, between better-known Boothbay Harbor and Camden. It's a region of thick stands of pine and white clapboard homes, where summer is as much a verb as a season, and long-term vacationers from Connecticut, Massachusetts, New York, and beyond populate the summer homes here as they have for generations. The river itself flows out of Damariscotta Lake and enters the Atlantic nineteen miles later. Much of the river is tidal, and in its lower reaches seems more a bay than a river. Part of the Damariscotta's allure for paddlers is the mix of different habitats to explore. Tom described a few different day-trip options.

"If you're more of a beginner, I'd suggest that you explore the inner reaches of the river. Near the village of South Bristol, there's a spot called The Gut—basically a little cove that's between Rutherford Island and the mainland. [Rutherford Island, part of South Bristol, is connected to the mainland by a swing bridge.] You can put in at The Gut and explore the island. If you head west, it will bring you to the Damariscotta. You'll head downstream, toward the ocean. You might decide to explore Christmas Cove, a wonderful protected bay that's home to a number of summer cottages. [It's said to have been discovered by a Captain John Smith on—you guessed it—Christmas Day in 1614.] Another option is to continue around Shipley Point (the island's tip) and circumnavigate Rutherford. As you round the tip, you'll come to a series of ledges called the Thread of Life. These were problematic for fishermen and sailors of another age. The story goes that men whose ships had wrecked on the rocks could jump from ledge to ledge to get to shore and safety. You head through the Thread of Life and continue north into John's Bay. Here, you're open to a little ocean swell, but you're still close to shore. You have an hour or so of more paddling before you reach the east entrance to The Gut. It's fun to pack a lunch and stop at Witch Island, just east of the entrance, for a picnic. The island is a wildlife sanctuary, and there's a nice little beach to land. In two or three hours, this loop gives you a little of everything coastal Maine has to offer—protected coves, a quaint lobster fishery, and a chance to see seals and osprey."

Tom also highlighted a path for seasoned paddlers seeking a more challenging outing. "I'd launch at The Gut again, but this time head due south out of the river mouth toward Fisherman Island. One option would be to circumnavigate the island, which has a substantial stone house, once the retreat of a prosperous Unitarian minister. Another option is to continue past Fisherman on to Damariscove Island. You can pull into a deep narrow harbor with a tidal cove. The island has a long history; sometimes you can find remnants of clay pipes from colonial times in the cove at low tide, and there are trails you can hike in the summer. [Thanks to its protected cove, Damariscove was used as a base for cod fishermen as early as 1608. It's said that the pilgrims who settled at Plymouth sailed to Damariscove in 1622, facing starvation; the fishermen provisioned them a boatful of cod. The island was later the site of a lifesaving station. Though privately owned now, the structure still stands.] After a picnic lunch at Damariscove, I'd head east and paddle past Outer Heron Island, then past White Island and back through the Thread of Life, along Rutherford Island, and back through The Gut. I have to stress that you need a good-weather day to do this route and an experienced crew. But this ocean exposure will be a great contrast to the inner-waters adventure.

"One of my happiest kayaking memories is paddling around Outer Heron Island in a double boat with my daughter Allie; she made her first trip out when she was six or seven. My wife, Liz, was with us in her single. We had a line in the water trolling for mackerel. A few times we had three fish on at the same time; it was a struggle to get them in while we were trying to paddle. It was a quintessential Maine experience—flat calm, blue sky, catching fish while we're trolling out of our kayaks, a bald eagle flying by. That sums up what you can experience. If you're lucky, you might even get to see a gannet [the largest seabird in the North Atlantic]. In this part of the world, they mostly roost up on Bonaventure Island, south of Quebec's Gaspé Peninsula. Sometimes they'll come this far south, and you'll see them around Outer Heron—a special surprise."

TOM ARMSTRONG is senior vice president and chief merchandising officer for L.L. Bean. He is an avid mountaineer, cyclist, cross-country skier, and sea kayaker. Tom has run the Mount Washington Road Race, participated in four Canadian ski marathons, and kayaked from New York City to the St. Lawrence River.

DESTINATION

25

If You Go

▶ **Getting There:** The greater Damariscotta region is approximately fifty miles north of Portland, which is served by many major carriers, including Delta (800-221-1212; www .delta.com) and United Airlines (800-864-8331; www.united.com).

▶ **Best Time to Visit:** Mid-June through September, with weather improving in August.

▶ **Guides/Outfitters:** Several companies serve the Damariscotta River region, including Midcoast Kayak (207-563-5732; www.midcoastkayak.com).

▶ **Level of Difficulty:** Paddles in the more sheltered sections of the river are fine for less seasoned paddlers; offshore paddles are only recommended for more advanced kayakers.

▶ **Accommodations:** Damariscotta, Boothbay, and Pemaquid Point have ample visitor accommodations, from B&Bs to hotels. The Maine Office of Tourism (888-624-6345; www.visitmaine.com) has a comprehensive list of options.

ST. CROIX RIVER

RECOMMENDED BY **Rob Scribner**

For earlier generations of Americans along the eastern seaboard, a trip to the wilderness meant a trip to northern Maine, an opportunity to be immersed in great pine forests and perhaps paddle a clear running river. The St. Croix still delivers on this promise.

"The St. Croix is a great spot to experience the Maine woods, and it's also an excellent river to develop your canoeing skills," Rob Scribner began. "There's a lot of white water, but it's easy white water; I like to describe it as lively but not intimidating. The water levels are regulated for recreational uses throughout the summer and fall, so there's always a decent amount of water. Some Maine rivers have runnable white water in the spring, but the water temps are 45°F. In the summer, the St. Croix can be in the seventies. Since the water is warm enough to swim in and the rapids aren't too scary, it's a great place to introduce people to the basics of white-water canoeing and camping. Plus, there's tremendous smallmouth bass fishing. Lots of folks come off the river after four days and say, 'That was great, we want to do another trip like the St. Croix.' Unfortunately, there aren't any other rivers like this . . . at least not in Maine."

The St. Croix River flows sixty-odd miles from its source in the Chiputneticook Lakes, a system that comprises North, East Grand, Mud, Spednic, and Palfrey Lakes, as well as numerous small feeder lakes. It forms much of the southern boundary between Maine and New Brunswick before it enters Passamaquoddy Bay and the Atlantic below the town of Calais. While the river can be run from Spednic Lake all the way to the salt (with a portage around Grand Falls Dam), most focus their efforts on the top thirty-three miles of the upper river, from the town of Vanceboro to Kellyland. Some will kayak the river, but most ply its waters with canoes. There's a rich canoeing heritage in the region; Old Town Canoe, opened its doors in 1898, just a few hours west in the village of Old Town.

OPPOSITE:
The rapids on the St. Croix are just challenging enough to help river canoeists expand their skills.

DESTINATION

26

"Some people want to make a week-long trip, but most put in at Vanceboro and take out at Kellyland, camping at sites that are nicely maintained by the St. Croix International Waterway Commission. If I'm out with a group of people that's new to river canoeing, I make the first day Paddling 101. There are lots of opportunities to instruct on the St. Croix. The features are there, but everything is Class I or II. I'll show people how to make an eddy turn, how to pole the canoe. By the time they get to Little Falls (rated a Class III in some guidebooks) on day two, they've got the basic tools to handle it. It's about two hundred yards long with several drops. I'll show people the line; if they follow it, they'll make it easy. (There's also the option to portage around.) It makes a nice little climax. Once you've paddled Little Falls, you feel like, 'Yeah, I can do this.' The other rapid that people think about is Canoose. It has one big drop that's actually bigger than the drops in Little Falls. As you approach Canoose, you can't see the drop; you're just looking over a horizon line. That's a little nerve-racking. If you start in the right spot and follow the line, you'll be good."

As you paddle the St. Croix, there are many opportunities for wildlife sightings, as well as fishing. "The best time to see moose in the summer is early morning or dusk," Rob said. "In the upper sections above Loon Bay, the river is fairly tight with lots of turns. If you're making a lot of noise, you can scare moose that are a few bends away. Below Loon Bay the river straightens out and widens a bit. You can make the moose out a half or a third mile away and then sneak up on them. We also see lots of whitetail deer, bald eagles and osprey. The top water fishing for smallmouth bass is loads of fun. As I'm drifting down, I'll cast over by spots where there's structure in the water. If you get your fly or lure where you want, chances are the water will erupt with a fish. I've had so many kids get their first fish on the St. Croix. I tell the kids, 'Give me forty-five minutes, and you'll catch a fish.'"

The north woods scenery on the St. Croix is striking at any time of year, but it's especially stunning in the early fall. "If you have the ability to [visit] in mid-September, you might have the river to yourself," Rob advised. "It's cooler for sleeping, and you can count on the foliage—the bright reds and oranges of the maples contrast with the yellow of the birch and poplars, all against the sea of green of the pines and firs." If you do canoe the St. Croix in the fall, you might want to go with a friend who doesn't snore—Rob elaborated: "I was camping with a client named Dick one night in early October," he recalled. "Our tents were pitched about a hundred yards apart. I woke up with a start in the morning, as the ground was shaking. I was a little groggy, and my first thought was that Dick was running up the trail from his tent to mine wearing big galoshes. About then, something hit one of the guidelines of my tent, and the thing shook. The fly of my tent was open a little, and I peeked out—I had a very close-up view of the nose of a bull moose and the tips of its antlers. It was a huge specimen, at least eight hundred pounds. I tried to get a picture, but it trotted away pretty fast. When I got up, I traced the hoof prints back to Dick's tent. I figured that the moose must have come out of the woods when he heard Dick snoring, thinking he'd found an eligible mate."

ROB SCRIBNER started guiding commercial river trips as summer work while attending the University of Maine in his hometown of Machias. He began guiding on his own in 1996, running primarily kayak trips. After graduating, Rob expanded his services to include guided canoe trips and outfitting services, establishing Sunrise Canoe and Kayak.

If You Go

▶ **Getting There:** Visitors can either fly into Portland (served by a number of carriers) or Bangor, which is served by Delta (800-221-1212; www.delta.com) and US Airways (800-428-4322; www.usairways.com).

▶ **Best Time to Visit:** The St. Croix can be run from May to October; prime time is July through mid-September.

▶ **Guides/Outfitters:** A number of outfitters lead trips on the St. Croix, including Sunrise Canoe and Kayak (877-980-2300; www.sunrisecanoeandkayak.com).

▶ **Level of Difficulty:** Beginners will be fine; this is a great spot to build your canoeing skills.

▶ **Accommodations:** Rob recommends the Machais Motor Inn (207-255-4861; www.machiasmotorinn.com or Bluebird Motel (207-255-3332) for guided trips or the Bellmard Inn (207-796-2261; www.bellmardinn.com) in Princeton for outfitted trips.

DESTINATION 26

CAMPECHE

RECOMMENDED BY **Michelle Bowman**

Michelle Bowman loves to surf, and she loves to fish. So when stand-up paddleboarding [SUP] skyrocketed to popularity, it was a natural fit. "Some fellow surfers and I would be out off the coast north of San Diego on days when the surf was flat," she began. "We'd be staring out at a kelp bed a little farther offshore, watching fish breach and flocks of birds diving on bait. One day someone asked, 'Why aren't we out there fishing?' Stand-up paddleboards weren't that accessible yet, and we didn't know about them, so we began bringing our longboards down to the beach. We'd paddle out to the kelp beds with our spinning rods. When SUPs came along, it was a no-brainer. You could paddle out and cast a spinning rod, but since it was more stable than our longboards, you could also fly-fish off of them. That was ideal for me, as I like fly-fishing better than gear fishing."

No water sport in recent memory has gained momentum as quickly as stand-up paddleboarding, where practitioners use a single-bladed paddle to propel an extralong (and slightly more buoyant than average) surfboard along. SUPs allow the maneuverability and shallow water clearance of kayaks and canoes, but afford the paddler a higher vantage point, allowing you to see below you as well as around you. The phenomenon appears to have materialized out of nowhere, though the practice dates back to the 1960s, when paddles were used by Hawaiian surf instructors to help newbies get the hang of standing up on a board. The same instructors would paddle themselves around when the surf was flat as a means of staying in shape. Several events sprang up around paddleboarding, including the Moloka'i to O'ahu Paddleboard Race in 1996, which helped bring the pastime visibility . . . though it was two surfer-entrepreneurs, Deb and Warren Thomas, who brought the first commercially available SUPs to market from their home in Santa Barbara.

OPPOSITE:
Michelle Bowman connects with a tarpon from the platform of her stand-up paddleboard in the mangroves of Campeche.

DESTINATION

27

"I feel that SUP is a great all-around workout," Michelle continued. "You keep your core engaged as you work to maintain your balance, and you work your upper body as you paddle . . . plus there's strength training from carrying the board around! When you throw fly-fishing into it, it's even better. You're not just looking straight ahead; sometimes you're casting to the sides or behind you. You need all of your muscles to stay afloat."

Ever since she first paddled out to the kelp beds off southern California with a spinning rod, Michelle had longed to take her paddleboard to the Caribbean or Gulf of Mexico to cast a fly for tarpon—one of fly-fishing's most prized game fish. Fortunately, she has a good inside connection for such endeavors in the shape of her husband, Conway Bowman, who has hosted several fly-fishing television programs over the years, including *Fly Fishing the World*. "When Conway announced that the show was going to be filming in Campeche, Mexico, and invited me to come along, I didn't hesitate."

Little known beyond the fly-fishing world (and not especially well-known there), Campeche sits midway down the western edge of the Yucatán Peninsula, on the Gulf of Mexico. Though rich in both Mayan archeological sites and Spanish colonial architecture (including a walled village dating from the late seventeenth century), the city is mostly overlooked by visitors who flock to the beaches and ruins to its southeast. It's not the city's history that attracted Conway and Michelle, but instead the countless miles of mangrove swamps, riddled with creeks and channels, that provide ideal nursery environs for tarpon. Tarpon have long been prized by anglers for their savage strikes and their incredible leaping availability. While these juvenile tarpon are a fraction of the size of the hundred-plus-pound behemoths that patrol the flats and reefs of the Caribbean (most are five to thirty pounds), they lack none of their elders' aggression. Few anglers will forget the first time they hooked a tarpon and the fish that jumped to their eye level, gills rattling . . . and often spitting the hook before they know what's hit them!

"Since I'd started fishing from a SUP, I knew it would be ideal for a place like Campeche," Michelle said. "The craft is perfectly apportioned for the situation. You can go into extremely shallow water, tuck easily underneath branches, and maneuver quietly around. With a SUP, you can get in places that boats simply can't get to.

"When I showed up at the dock with my board, the guide who was driving the panga didn't look too hopeful. I'm fairly sure he hadn't guided a SUPer before. We made our way out to the mangroves with a camera crew in tow. We maneuvered into a little mangrove channel, which then opened up into a lagoon, and there were fish breaching all over.

"Almost every fish I cast to went for the fly. These fish were hungry, and they're not cast to very often. I lost a few. It was the fourth or fifth fish I hooked that I was able to get to hand. The guide had suggested I paddle through a gap in the mangroves, and I saw some fish rolling at the far end of the lagoon. I paddled over slowly, made the cast, stripped the fly, and it stopped . . . and soon after, the fish jumped. Because the SUP is so light, you end up going wherever the fish goes. The tarpon I hooked went right toward the mangroves. I sat down on my board and used my legs to back paddle so I could move the fish toward the middle of the lagoon, away from the roots where it could bust my leader. I was spinning around as the fish kept jumping, but I eventually got it in."

MICHELLE BOWMAN'S passion for fishing began on a date with her husband, who asked if she wanted to learn how to fly fish. One eighty-pound mako later she was hooked! As a marine biologist in San Diego, Michelle blends her work life with her downtime by spending as much time on the water as possible. She often rises before dawn to get a few hours of fishing or surfing in before work. When not in the office, she travels with her husband and son on outdoor adventures around Southern California and beyond. She is sponsored in her SUP fishing efforts by Orvis, Hobie Stand Up Paddleboards, and Columbia Sportswear.

DESTINATION

27

If You Go

▶ **Getting There:** Continental (800-523-3273; www.continental.com) flies into Merida via Houston; Merida is an hour-and-a-half ride from Campeche. Or you can fly into Cancun, which is a five-and-a-half-hour drive from Campeche.

▶ **Best Time to Visit:** The mangroves around Campeche fish well throughout the year, though visitors may want to avoid hurricane season in early fall.

▶ **Guides/Outfitters:** There are several outfitters who fish Campeche, including Tarpon Town (+521 981 133 2135; www.tarpontown.com).

▶ **Level of Difficulty:** Conditions are user friendly, though casting a fly rod while on a stand-up paddleboard takes practice.

▶ **Accommodations:** There are a number of hotels available. Michelle stayed at Ocean View Hotel (+52 (981)8119991 - 99; www.oceanview.com.mx).

SEA OF CORTEZ

RECOMMENDED BY **Nancy Mertz**

Though Loreto and the crystalline waters of the Sea of Cortez (also known as the Gulf of California) are but a short plane ride from Los Angeles, they seem a world away. "It's almost too good to be true," Nancy Mertz opined. "The air is clean and pristine, the water is an incredible turquoise, and the geology is spectacular. When you're on the water, you might come upon leaping manta rays, seals, or whales at any moment. There are legions of colorful fish below the surface when you go snorkeling at lunch. Onshore, there are great hikes that take you to seldom-explored patches of desert flora and hidden washes that host a variety of animal life. At night, the number of stars is dizzying."

Baja California is a peninsula that extends 660 miles south from the California border. It's bounded on the east by the Sea of Cortez, which separates the peninsula from the rest of Mexico; to the west is the Pacific. The terrain of Baja is quite mountainous, crisscrossed by four major ranges—Sierra Juárez, Sierra de San Pedro Mártir, Sierra de la Giganta, and Sierra de la Laguna. The mountains serve to divert the little moisture that flows over the peninsula, rendering the region quite arid. While at times stark, Baja is a land of rich contrasts—not only the wet and the dry, but also the tremendous colors. The juxtaposition of the tropical greens and turquoises of the sea and sky with the ochre of the mountains and the pink and gold sands of the beaches is positively startling. Baja California is not undiscovered, but most winter sun-seekers flock to the rather Americanized resort towns of Cabo San Lucas and San Jose del Cabo at the southern tip of the peninsula. The country between Loreto and La Paz, which begins roughly two-thirds of the way down the peninsula on the Sea of Cortez, is relatively undeveloped, with nary a Señor Frog's in sight.

Many of Nancy's kayaking adventures on the Sea of Cortez have begun near the city of Loreto. From this charming colonial city (first established in 1697 by Jesuit missionaries), there are a number of options. One is to circumnavigate the island of Carmen in the Loreto Bay National Marine Park, a sixty-mile paddle over nine days; another is to paddle the sixty-five-mile roadless coast from Loreto to La Paz over ten days. An expedition that has appeal for kayakers of all skill levels is a multiday tour of the inner islands of Loreto Bay. This option showcases everything that makes Baja one of North America's great sea kayaking destinations, with more modest mileage between campsites.

"We generally visit two islands in Loreto Bay—Danzante and Carmen," Nancy continued, "and camp a few days at each spot. Danzante, our first stop, is a fairly short paddle— roughly an hour. The park service assigns us a beach to camp on. Beyond that, our itinerary is very flexible. We'll do paddles each day to visit other nearby islands and visit good snorkeling spots. In camp, there are lots of hiking opportunities. Many of our guides are biology students from the university in La Paz, and they are eager to introduce guests to the plants and animals that make up the island ecology. During the time spent around camp, some will choose to just swim and snooze in the sand. The sunsets are spectacular, and we offer fresh margaritas to go with the view. We make sure coffee is ready for early risers who want to take in the sunrises, which are equally great." (Both self-supported and boat-supported excursions are available.)

Though Isla Danzante and Carmen have many appeals—the vistas from the headlands of volcanic rock juxtaposing towering cacti with the sea are otherworldly—the main show takes place on the water. Many whales pass part of their winter here—fins, humpbacks, minke, and blue whales. Blue whales are the largest animal ever to swim or walk the earth and can reach lengths of over ninety feet and weights of 170 tons—which is to say, many times the size of your kayak. Biologists believe that whales show up here to feed on crustaceans that thrive in the fertile waters of the Sea of Cortez. "The blue whales like deeper water, and they are generally moving through, not lollygagging around," Nancy said. "You see them most frequently when you're making crossings between islands. You'll be paddling along and a huge black back will appear. Soon you'll hear the sound of a spout. It seems like it's right next to you, but the area is so quiet, the whales are actually half a mile away. The guides love to show people the whales. They seem to have eyes in the backs of their heads and will stop anything they're doing to get guests out to encounter them. Back in the early nineties, we wouldn't see that many whales, blue or other species. It's amazing how they've come back since hunting (mostly by Japanese whalers) was

DESTINATION

28

significantly curtailed. Whale sharks are also being seen more and more frequently. Early in the season, they're closer to La Paz, but they move toward Loreto later in the spring.

"I was first drawn to Baja over twenty years ago by my love of kayaking and my fascination with whales," Nancy added. "If I only had one trip I could do in Baja, I'd want to head down in early March and spend five days kayaking on the Sea of Cortez, searching for fin and blue whales, and then three days on Magdalena Bay on the Pacific side of the peninsula, where gray whales calve. You can't kayak with the whales on Magdalena Bay, but even from a boat, the whale babies are fat and sassy. The gray whale babies actually approach the pangas. They are so curious that they swim right up to the boat to gaze back at whale watchers. You can reach out to touch them, and they don't flinch. It's an unforgettable experience."

OPPOSITE: Desert meets ocean as lone paddlers explores Honeymoon Cove on Danzante Island.

NANCY MERTZ formed Sea Kayak Adventures with her husband, Terry Prichard, after first meeting in Baja California in the early nineties. She's been a sea kayak guide for many years in Baja and the Pacific Northwest, including British Columbia's Johnstone Strait. She also guided on Idaho's white-water rivers in the summer through ROW Adventures. In 2012, Sea Kayak Adventures became part of the ROW Adventures family of companies.

DESTINATION

28

If You Go

▶ **Getting There:** Many kayak adventures stage in Loreto, which is served by Alaska Airlines (800-252-7522; www.alaskaair.com) via Los Angeles.

▶ **Best Time to Visit:** Novice kayakers will want to avoid the north winds, which are prevalent December through February. October, November, March, and April are the best months for beginners.

▶ **Guides/Outfitters:** Many companies lead kayaking trips in Baja, including Sea Kayak Adventures (800-616-1943; www.seakayakadventures.com).

▶ **Level of Difficulty:** With the exception of its windy season, Baja is well suited to less seasoned kayakers.

▶ **Accommodations:** Baja Life Online (loreto.com) lists a range of lodging options in town.

BOUNDARY WATERS

RECOMMENDED BY **Bill Forsberg**

A paddle cuts the tea-colored water of a North Country lake. Thick hardwoods encircle the water. The quiet is broken by the eerie and at once unmistakable cry of a loon. A bull moose, previously undetected against a fallen maple near the shoreline, lifts its massive head from the lake where it was feeding on water lilies and shakes, sending a halo of droplets into the last rays of sunlight.

Welcome to the Boundary Waters of Minnesota.

"People refer to this area as 'God's Country,'" Bill Forsberg began, "and I can't think of a better way to describe it. Man hasn't come in and messed it up. When you're paddling these waters, you're traveling the same paths as the voyageurs [the French-Canadian fur traders who were the first Europeans to visit the region]. A few days here is an opportunity to get to nature, the simplicity of life."

The Boundary Waters Canoe Area is a wilderness area in northeastern Minnesota, along the boundary with Ontario. The one million acres of the BWCA—deep forests of mixed conifers and hardwoods, lakes large and small, and rivers that connect many of the lakes—fall in the Superior National Forest and comprise the largest wilderness preserve east of the Rocky Mountains. The Boundary Waters are joined on the Ontario side by Quetico Provincial Park, another million acres of wilderness. Overall, the BWCA contains over a thousand lakes, most carved out by the glacial activity of the Canadian Shield. Bill estimates that there are some 1,500 miles of "official" canoe trails in the Boundary Waters, and more than two thousand wilderness campsites.

"Considering all the different places you can launch from and all the areas you can explore," Bill continued, "there are options for whatever kind of experience people are seeking, whatever their ability levels. There's a great deal of variance out there in terms of

OPPOSITE:
There are more
than one million
wilderness acres
to explore in
the Boundary
Waters
Canoe Area.

DESTINATION

29

habitat. You might start on a modest creek or river and then portage into a small lake down in a boggy area. The next portage might take you to a vast lake with high bluffs. Some folks want to get out into the wilderness, set up a base camp, fish surrounding waters, and kick back. Other people want to see a new lake every day and are eager to see what's around the next portage. Many trips are planned for five or six days, with paddlers covering six to eight miles a day. More adventurous canoeists might stay out for ten days or two weeks and cover ten to twelve miles a day."

As Bill mentioned, fishing is certainly a significant part of a Boundary Waters expedition for many who come here. Lake trout are present in some of the waters, panfish, too. But most anglers are more interested in northern pike, walleye, and smallmouth bass. Pike are long and narrow with a mouth full of sharp teeth and are known for their lack of inhibition when it comes to taking a bait or lure; they fry or grill well. Walleye are celebrated for their fine taste and are the target species for anglers more interested in a nice camp meal than a good battle. For many serious anglers, smallmouth are the prime target—they're scrappy fighters and just particular enough to pose a challenge. "Out in the Boundary Waters, you have a legitimate chance at trophy fish, whatever you're targeting," Bill added. "It depends, of course, on the angler's ability, the weather . . . and, a little luck. Though I'm an avid walleye angler, I think it's hard to beat smallmouth."

Moose are another totemic appeal of the North Woods. The largest member of the deer family, these gangly creatures can reach weights of more than a thousand pounds and stand six feet at the shoulder. In the Boundary Waters, moose are generally encountered in lakes or marshes, where they can chomp up to a hundred pounds of lilies and wild rice a day. Though they appear cartoonishly awkward and are generally docile, it's wise to keep a healthy distance—especially from males during the fall rut and females with calves in early spring—as an angry moose can inflict fatal damage with its hooves. Bill shared a nonlethal (but fairly funny) encounter: "I was out paddling on the Little Isabella River with a friend of mine from college who hadn't spent much time in the wilderness. As we came around a bend, there was a brown lump of fur blocking the river. I thought it was a bear at first. The lump wasn't much more than six feet in front of the canoe when a cow moose lifted up its head. I was reaching for my camera as my friend screamed and threw his paddle . . . the moose was unfazed and meandered off." (The BWCA has some of Minnesota's most robust moose populations, roughly five thousand animals . . . in addition to deer, bears, mink, otter, lynx, wolverine, and wolves.)

If paddlers have any hesitations about the Boundary Waters, they can be summed up in two words: portaging and mosquitoes. While both are part of the experience, they're generally not as bad as you might suspect. "Most people think of portaging as two people carrying a canoe over their heads like they see on a TV commercial," Bill said. "We use yolk pads, and one person carries the boat. Our Kevlar canoes weigh only forty-two pounds. The biggest thing to take into consideration is what you're going to bring. Some people show up with coolers and big stoves, like they're going car camping. They forget they have to carry all of this stuff. You need to think more like you're going on a backpacking trip. As far as the bugs are concerned, people envision them being so much worse than they really are. It's true that springtime has its share of mosquitoes, and you want to be prepared. But they generally diminish as the season goes on."

Night comes late in the summer in the Boundary Waters. Yet it's worth staying up. "The number of stars is amazing," Bill added. "There's just no light pollution."

BILL FORSBERG operates Boundary Waters Outfitters in Ely, Minnesota. He's canoed the vast majority of Minnesota's Boundary Waters and Canada's Quetico Provincial Park and is an avid angler.

If You Go

▶ **Getting There:** Many Boundary Waters trips stage in Ely, which is a four-hour drive north of Minneapolis.

▶ **Best Time to Visit:** May through early October. Bugs are lighter later in the season.

▶ **Guides/Outfitters:** A number of outfitters cater to BWCA travelers, including Boundary Waters Outfitters (800-777-8574; www.boundarywatersoutfitters.com). They can provide do-it-yourselfers with all the gear and guidance they need.

▶ **Level of Difficulty:** While the paddling required is not technical, visitors should be in decent physical condition to perform necessary portages.

▶ **Accommodations:** Timber Trail Lodge & Resort (800-777-8574; www.timbertrail lodge.com) provides simple lodging near where most trips originate.

UPPER MIDDLE FORK FLATHEAD RIVER

RECOMMENDED BY **Mike Cooney**

As Glacier National Park may be destined to forever play second fiddle to Yellowstone among Montana's national parks, the Middle Fork Flathead River may always linger in the shadows of another Middle Fork river in Idaho . . . though many believe it's equally worthy of attention.

"The Middle Fork is considered one of the best white-water rivers in Montana," Mike Cooney began. "It's a designated Wild and Scenic river, and in its upper reaches, there are only two ways to get in: hiking with horses or mules, or flying. It's as pristine and crystal clear a river as you'll find in the lower forty-eight, flowing free and undammed, all created by Mother Nature. I've run the Middle Fork more than a hundred times, and every time, it's a new river. It changes with every inch of water that drains in." [The National Wild and Scenic Rivers Act of 1968 was enacted to place restraints on development along rivers and limits the number of boaters allowed on a river each day, helping to ensure a quality wilderness experience.]

The Middle Fork rises in the Bob Marshall Wilderness Area, south of Glacier National Park, and flows roughly ninety miles in a northwesterly direction, eventually forming the southern border of the park. Near the towns of West Glacier and Columbia Falls, it joins the North Fork to form the main stem of the Flathead. The heart of its Wild and Scenic section tumbles through the Great Bear Wilderness, where stands of lodgepole pine extend thousands of feet up glacier-carved valleys, and snowcapped mountains pierce the sky well into July. Given its mountainous terrain and the general absence of human influence, the area is a haven for many of the northern Rockies' totemic mammals, including moose, elk, mountain goat, black bear, wolverine, lynx, bighorn sheep—and one of the highest population densities of grizzly bear south of Alaska. (Just beyond the take-out,

OPPOSITE:
Much of the incredibly clear Middle Fork flows through the heart of the Great Bear Wilderness.

DESTINATION

30

there's a spot called Goat Lick where you have an excellent chance of spying mountain goat.) It's the thirty-five miles of the Middle Fork running from Schafer Meadows to Bear Creek that are of greatest interest to paddlers. This section offers two distinct seasons—big white water (June) and more technical, wilderness floats (July to late August). Mike described the two experiences.

"In June, the Middle Fork is a solid Class IV river. In its upper reaches, it's dropping sixty-eight feet a mile, so you can imagine that it's moving pretty good. There's still a lot of snow in the higher country, so the only way you can get in there is to take a small plane into Schafer Meadows. We usually run the river down to Bear Creek over the next three and a half days. This gives us time to scout and run the bigger rapids along the way and also provides time for some great day hikes and kicking back around camp. We generally run the river in paddle rafts, and everyone in the boat really needs to work together to get through smoothly. There are a couple of rapids that are always interesting in the upper section of this float. The first is Three Forks, which has several named drops—Lover's Leap, Rock 'n' Roll, and Last Drop. Of these, Last Drop is the most challenging. It's a ledge drop that stretches across the river. When it's high water, there's a massive hole here. If you're not right on your line, you're going swimming. Spruce Park is another favorite. One drop here is called Five Card Draw. It comes after a blind corner; if you're not on the left, you're in for a major swim. I was running it one time and watched one of the other guides get ejected fifteen feet in the air as his raft hit Five Card Draw. He was telling his crew, 'All forward!' and then he was airborne.

Since you're only covering thirty-five miles, there's time on a June float to include a few hikes that let you experience the grandeur of the Great Bear Wilderness from a different perspective. "One hike is up to Scott Lake," Mike said. "It's about two to two and a half hours. There are often moose up there, as well as relics of turn-of-the-century trapper's dwellings . . . though you have to know what you're looking for. Another short hike—about an hour—is up to Castle Lake. It has some incredible early season trout fishing. Two other hikes—Vinegar Mountain and Spruce Point—get you up on top of the world, with views over the Great Bear, the Bob, and even into Glacier. On all the hikes the wildflowers are amazing."

As snowmelt diminishes, the Middle Fork takes on a different, though still pleasing, character. "When you get to July, the ten miles below Schafer Meadows are too low to run smoothly," Mike explained, "so we put in at a spot called Granite Creek. It's about a two-hour hike in, and we carry the rafts and supplies with horses and mules. People who float at this time of year are either looking for a wilderness experience or a chance to fish. There are still some good rapids to run, though they're more technical in nature. Sometimes we'll run inflatable kayaks."

The fly-fishing on the Middle Fork can be incredible. All the trout in the river are native—primarily westslope cutthroat, with some bull trout as well. The cutthroat are eager to rise to a variety of dry flies. Sometimes it hardly seems to matter what anglers attach to their leader. "On the Middle Fork, a competent angler can expect to catch and release 40 to 50 fish on an average day," Mike added. "I once had a client land 138 in one outing."

MIKE COONEY is a lead guide and operations manager for Glacier Raft Company/ Glacier Angler. A fifth-generation Montanan, he first ran the Middle Fork with his family at age thirteen and has worked at Glacier Raft Company since 1990. In addition to being a white-water guide, he's a mule packer and fishing guide.

If You Go

▶ **Getting There:** Visitors can fly to Kalispell (twenty-five miles south of Glacier), which is served by Alaska Airlines (800-252-7522; www.alaskaair.com) and United Airlines (800-864-8331; www.united.com).

▶ **Best Time to Visit:** June is white-water time; July and August is for fishing/wilderness floats.

▶ **Guides/Outfitters:** Glacier Raft Company (800-235-6781; www.glacierraftco.com) is the only Montana-based company permitted to lead trips on the Upper Middle Fork.

▶ **Level of Difficulty:** Inexperienced paddlers will be fine on guided trips if you're in good health; only advanced rafters/kayakers should consider the Middle Fork on their own, especially in June.

▶ **Accommodations:** Glacier Raft Company has lodging. The Flathead Convention & Visitor Bureau (800-543-3105; www.fcvb.org) highlights other options.

ABEL TASMAN NATIONAL PARK

RECOMMENDED BY **Jack Kelly**

New Zealand's South Island is renowned for its remarkable hiking trails. The Routeburn and Milford Tracks draw trekkers from around the world. Another trail of sorts of equal merit can be found near the South Island's northern tip, off Abel Tasman National Park.

"I think the main appeal of Abel Tasman is the tremendous beauty and diversity of habitat that's found in a short space," Jack Kelly said. "In thirty or thirty-five miles, you'll come upon incredible golden beaches, imposing rocky headlands, and river estuaries and lagoons filled with clear water and thriving with life, including New Zealand fur seals. In places, thick forests fringe right down to the shoreline, creating a vivid contrast of green, gold, and blue. Nearly all the paddling is in a bay, so there are no big swells. The park is very accessible. You'll see three-year-olds and grandparents out in the park, and everyone in between, and there's a great mix of paddles—half day, single day, multiday."

Peter Jackson's *Lord of the Rings* trilogy showed the world what many Kiwis and avid outdoors people already knew—that the southern island of New Zealand is an area of incomparable natural beauty. The combination of steep mountains, dark green forests, snowcapped peaks, foaming waterfalls, and fingers of blue fjords make the region one of the most visually stunning temperate areas in the world. Abel Tasman National Park's wonders are on a bit of a smaller scale but are nonetheless beguiling. The park extends form Wainui Inlet in the north to Marahau in the south and includes the waters of the Tonga Island Marine Reserve. Though Abel Tasman is New Zealand's smallest national park, it is its most used, visited by over 150,000 hikers, beachgoers, campers, and kayakers each year. Jack's favorite way to experience Abel Tasman is to mix a day's walk with several days of paddling.

OPPOSITE: The many ecosystems you'll encounter in a day's paddle of Abel Tasman make it a special venue.

DESTINATION

31

"We start at Golden Bay at the northern end of the park," he explained, "and begin on foot. We move north to south, as that's the course of the prevailing winds. This section of coastline is stunning and sees fewer visitors than other parts of the park. The day's hike takes us around one of the main granite headlands, Separation Point. There's a significant New Zealand fur seal colony here, and you can hike down to observe them. We continue to Anapai Beach, where we'll camp for the night. During this first day, visitors are soaking up the feel of the place. The second day, we'll hike a few more miles down to Totaranui Beach, an iconic New Zealand camping spot. [Totaranui is one of the best examples of Abel Tasman's unique golden sand, a result of deposits of quartz crystals.] Water taxis meet us here and drop off our kayaks. For the rest of the trip, we're in our boats."

Visitors have the next three days to explore twenty-five-odd miles of coastline. The finishing point for the first day of paddling is Onetahuti Beach, a half-moon-shaped, one-kilometer-long expanse of sand. One of the highlights en route is Shag Harbor. "You enter the harbor via a tiny entrance through a rocky headland," Jack continued. "If you didn't know it was here, you'd go right past it. The water's very clear, and the lagoon has a golden bottom. There are usually lots of fur seals swimming about. Moving south on the second day of paddling, you come into the heart of the park, with many river estuaries and lagoons. The flora and overall feel are very different from the park's northern reaches; it looks like a totally different world. On full tide, we can paddle into the lagoons where the forests extend right down to the water." The forests and scrub are home to some of New Zealand's endemic birds, including tui, bellbird, and kereru. A host of water birds like shags, oyster catchers, herons, and pukeko (purple swamp hen) are found near estuaries and lagoons. Life below the lagoon is equally inviting. Pink algae coats many of the rocks, providing a colorful backdrop for a host of smaller creatures, ranging from periwinkles, tubeworms, Neptune's necklace (also known as sea grapes), sea urchins, and Cook's turban shells.

There are a number of diverting walks one can take from camp at Anchorage Bay. You can hike to the overlook at Te Pukatea Bay, which provides vistas all the way across Tasman Bay. Or you can visit Cleopatra's Pool, a freshwater swimming hole that comes with a moss-lined, natural waterslide. Another nearby attraction is a glowworm cave, lit by thousands of *Arachnocampa luminosa*, an iridescent worm endemic to New Zealand. There's one more day of paddling to complete your tour of Abel Tasman. "The first hour or so, we head around a rocky headland called the Mad Mile," Jack continued. "The wind can come up in the afternoon, hence the name. But in the morning, it's fine. After the Mad Mile, we'll do a brief crossing out to Adele Island. Native bird species have been reintroduced to the island as part of a joint initiative between local commercial business operators, local volunteers, and the Department of Conservation. You can sit on the beach, close your eyes, and listen to an avian symphony. It's a magical spot. From Adele, we head back to Marahau, near the southern end of the park. If the breeze comes up, we'll hoist a spinnaker sail and let the wind take us in the last two or three miles. The route takes us through an estuary of more golden beaches. Snowcapped mountains are in the distance."

JACK KELLY has been kayaking and walking the Abel Tasman coastline since he was a kid. Family holidays were a boat ride into the park and weeks spent playing on the water and running around beaches and sand flats and in the native forest. Some things don't change, and it was these early experiences that were the inspiration for Jack's founding Marahau Sea Kayaks in 2001 and, more recently, putting the iconic Abel Tasman Kayaks back into local hands by purchasing it back from the big guys. He shares his days with a fantastic crew of New Zealand kayak guides.

If You Go

▶ **Getting There:** Most visitors will fly into Nelson, which is served via Auckland, Christchurch, and Wellington by Air New Zealand (+64 9 357 3000; www.airnewzealand .co.nz). Marahau, near Abel Tasman National Park, is a ninety-minute drive from Nelson.

▶ **Best Time to Visit:** Most visitors paddle between October and mid-April, with the austral summer being the busiest season.

▶ **Guides/Outfitters:** Many outfitters lead trips in the waters of Abel Tasman, including Abel Tasman Kayaks (+64 3 527 8022; www.abeltasmankayaks.co.nz).

▶ **Level of Difficulty:** New paddlers will feel comfortable on the waters around Abel Tasman.

▶ **Accommodations:** New Zealand Tourism (www.newzealand.com) lists lodging options around the park for before or after your paddling excursion.

DESTINATION

31

NAHANNI RIVER

RECOMMENDED BY **Neil Hartling**

If you live south of the Canadian border, you may not have heard of the Nahanni. But odds are good that if you hail from Toronto, Calgary, or Vancouver, you know it as Canada's iconic wilderness river.

"Among many canoeists and rafters, running the Nahanni is a pilgrimage, a trip that seems larger than life, too big to grasp," Neil Hartling enthused. "It takes you to Canada's biggest waterfall, through its deepest canyons, past hot springs and unique geologic features. All this transpires in one of the largest national parks in the world. When I was fifteen, I read a book called *Nahanni* by an adventurer named Dick Turner. Turner's book made a profound impression on me. It would take eight years, but I eventually got a chance to travel down the Nahanni. That was thirty years ago. Now I've been down fifty times, and I still marvel at the understated way he described his experience."

The Nahanni River begins in the Selwyn Mountains along the border of the Yukon and Northwest Territories, and it flows through the Mackenzie Mountains for some 350 miles in a southerly direction, along the southwestern border of the two territories until it reaches the Liard River. Nearly the entire river lies within Nahanni National Park Reserve, which, at 1,840 square miles, is larger than Switzerland. Most paddlers begin their float at Virginia Falls; from here, it's roughly 150 miles to the take-out, which is generally covered over a one-week or twelve-day float. (Above Virginia Falls there are some flat-water sections of the Nahanni that can be incorporated into a longer trip that is ideal for beginners; skilled paddlers can also incorporate the headwaters into a float.) Part of the Nahanni's iconic status in Canada stems from a visit by former prime minister Pierre Elliott Trudeau, who paddled the river in 1970. "This was before the popularity of ecotourism and adventure travel, and it was an unusual thing for a politician to be out in

OPPOSITE:
Explorations
of the Nahanni
have a memo-
rable beginning
at the towering
Virginia Falls.

DESTINATION

32

145

the wilderness," Neil added. Trudeau's trip thrust the region into the limelight and helped build momentum for the establishment of the national park.

The adventure begins before you've even set a paddle in the water. "The flight from Fort Simpson is one of the highlights of a trip with many highlights," Neil continued. "You fly over the Mackenzie Valley, a broad floodplain where you can see the striations in the ground where the glaciers pushed through. It's laid out like a classroom experiment in geology. Soon you hit the front range of the Mackenzie Mountains and glide over Little Doctor Lake, which rests in a small gap in the range. There are tremendous peaks on either side that seem to shoot up out of the lake. The next landmark is Ram Plateau, an immense karst landform that's slowly dissolving; its sides drop off dramatically. Now we begin following the river, up past the canyons. Finally, we reach Sunblood Mountain and Virginia Falls. The pilot circles the falls a few times before landing.

"When people step out of the plane next to the falls, they often say, 'That was so dramatic if the trip ended now, it would be worth the money.' I tell them it will just keep getting better, but they don't believe me. At the end, they say, 'You know, it just gets better.'"

Things start with a bang—or, should we say, a splash. Virginia Falls plummets 315 feet—nearly twice the height of Niagara Falls—and stretches some 850 feet from end to end. "It's a place of incredible natural power," Neil said. "You could spend days hanging out there, exploring the falls from different angles. We like to take at least a day. One option is to canoe across the river and hike up Sunblood Mountain. From the top, you get a 360-degree view, taking in the falls and the Mackenzie Mountains. If you're quiet, you have a good chance to see Dall sheep." After portaging gear around the falls, you'll begin making your way downriver, drinking in the wonders of the Nahanni's four canyons. In Third Canyon, some of the walls reach nearly 4,000 feet; halfway through this canyon, you reach The Gate and Pulpit Rock. Here, the canyon narrows to just over 100 yards, and the walls still tower 1,500 feet high. "There's a short hike you can do to the top of The Gate," Neil continued. "From there, it's quite a dramatic view of Pulpit Rock and the narrow gorge. When we float through, everyone is instinctively quiet so they can take it all in. It has a cathedral-like feeling.

"After Second Canyon, we reach Deadmen Valley. The skeletons of two brothers, Frank and Willie McLeod, were found here in 1908 at the edge of a creek. Their skulls had been removed; the creek is called Headless Creek. The valley is ringed by mountains, and it has a brooding, foreboding mood to it. Strong thermal activity causes frequent windstorms. Leaving Deadmen Valley, you float through George's Riffle. Riffle is an understatement—it's a jarring introduction to First Canyon, the deepest of the four canyons. There's a sense of majesty here and several great beaches for camping and taking it all in. One is called Coliseum, another Cathedral. A park planner couldn't have done it better. Before you leave the canyons, you reach Kraus Hotsprings, a great spot to recount stories from upriver. It's named for Gus Kraus, a homesteader. When Trudeau came through in 1970, he and Kraus had a conversation. The prime minister asked what Kraus would think if the place became a national park. He replied, 'Well, we were already thinking of leaving, as it's getting crowded. Last year twelve people came by.'"

As you float downriver, you're likely to encounter big game as well as big views. Inhabitants include moose, black and grizzly bears, and mountain caribou. The wildflowers can be overwhelming. "You think of the north as hostile to flowers, but the ground is invariably carpeted with them," Neil added. "And since it's summer, you have unlimited sunlight to explore late into the evening. You never have to be in a rush to get back to camp, and you can read a book at midnight without a flashlight."

The Nahanni has many sights to behold. Yet you needn't be sighted to appreciate its wonders.

"One time, we had a guest who was completely blind," Neil recalled. "He was a brilliant man, the CEO of the Canadian National Institute for the Blind [now known as CNIB]. I'll always remember how he interacted with the environment, the cues he picked up on. He knew when we were in a canyon—the speed of the current, the smells, the subtle changes in humidity and wind. Observing how he perceived this visually stunning place added another dimension for me."

NEIL HARTLING is an outfitter, guide, and educator and the author of three books of northern rivers. He founded Nahanni River Adventures in 1985 after rescuing a First Nations family on the river. The resulting relationship led to permission from the band to outfit and guide on the Nahanni, a privilege bestowed on few. His company is now both a successful eco-adventure company and a powerful platform for conservation. Neil is driven by the conviction that people will protect what they love. He provided leadership in the expansion of Nahanni National Park, protecting the Greater Nahanni Watershed and making it one of the largest parks in the world. Nahanni River Adventures has won the

DESTINATION

32

Yahoo! Big Idea Chair Award for the "Best Tourism Website in Canada" (www.nahanni .com), and has been designated by *National Geographic* as one of the "Best Adventure Travel Companies on Earth" and, in 2010, one of the "50 Tours of a Lifetime." The company now operates on twenty rivers across the north, and Neil likes to say that a bad day on the river is better than a good day doing anything else.

If You Go

▶ **Getting There:** First Air (800-267-1247; www.firstair.ca) offers flights to Fort Simpson, the staging area for Nahanni floats.

▶ **Best Time to Visit:** Neil likes to run the Nahanni June through August.

▶ **Guides/Outfitters:** Canadian River Expeditions (800-297-6927; www.nahanni.com) has been leading a variety of trips on the Nahanni since 1984.

▶ **Level of Difficulty:** Rafters traveling with an outfitter don't need previous paddling experience; canoeists need at least intermediate white-water skills.

▶ **Accommodations:** The Village of Fort Simpson (www.fortsimpson.com) lists lodging options for the beginning and end of your trip.

CAPE GARGANTUA (LAKE SUPERIOR)

RECOMMENDED BY **Joanie McGuffin**

Thirty years later, Joanie McGuffin vividly recalls the first time she saw Cape Gargantua. "It was 1983. My husband, Gary, and I, newly married, were in the midst of a cross-Canada canoe trip. Inspired by the history and geography of our country's waterways, we had mapped out an east-to-west route that linked beluga whale calving grounds in the St. Lawrence with the great Mackenzie River flowing into the Arctic Ocean. Among the maps of traditional North American trade routes, historical journals, and contemporary reads that provided impetus for the journey was a photography book entitled *Superior: The Haunted Shore* by Wayland Drew and Bruce Littlejohn. I remember this as the only coffee-table book in the home where I grew up. In the planning of our long voyage, Lake Superior was a highlight, though many of our friends were nervous about us paddling there. After all, many mariners feel traveling on Superior is more dangerous than navigating across the Atlantic Ocean. Two months into our cross-Canada voyage, we arrived in Sault Sainte Marie, where the Soo Locks raised us twenty feet to the height of Lake Superior. I must admit that it was with trepidation, and Gordon Lightfoot's 'The Wreck of the Edmund Fitzgerald' playing in our minds, that we paddled out onto the greatest Great Lake.

"Fear drove us to fourteen-hour days of paddling. (Our minds conjured images of November gales taking thousand-foot freighters to watery graves.) We dutifully followed the advice we had been given by well-meaning experts: *Get up at the crack of dawn and take advantage of the morning calm*. So in just ten days, we covered five hundred miles around the North Shore, paddling all the way from Whitefish Bay to the Pigeon River. My impressions, blurred by the exhaustion of this marathon, were of vast water meeting the horizon, beaches arcing into distant headlands, and precipitous cliffs plunging into dark depths. En route, we traversed Cape Gargantua. The mainland jutting into the lake was

fringed with dark, volcanic islands. Ancient cedars overhung sculptured shoals. Pockmarked gargoyles in twisted shapes, hidden grottos, whispering streams, and so much more left a strong impression. We yearned to return.

"Six years later, we did. This time we were on a summer-long circumnavigation of Lake Superior. After six weeks of paddling counterclockwise along the Minnesota, Wisconsin, and Michigan shores, we crossed Whitefish Bay and headed north once again into Ontario waters on Superior's eastern side. At the north end of Agawa Bay, we revisited the hundred-foot-high wall famous as a rock canvas embellished with dozens of pictographs. These ancient red ochre paintings depicting creatures like Misshepeshu, the spiny-back feline; sea serpents; canoes; and various figures reminded us of the thousands of years of Anishinaabe occupation of these lands and waters. Much of the paddling en route to Gargantua (twenty miles farther north) offers little protection from the three-hundred-mile fetch of open water until you reach the screen of small islands at Gargantua. This sheltered oasis on an otherwise exposed coast is something that would not have gone unnoticed by travelers through the centuries. These islands have always held great spiritual significance for the Anishinaabe people. It has been a place of excellent fishing, medicinal plant harvesting, nesting falcons, and red ochre gathering. Every time I travel through Gargantua, I have this feeling of many eyes upon me. Perhaps it is just the volcanic geology—dark brown and reddish in color—that feels primitive and alive, like the lava just cooled yesterday. But to me, the silhouetted figures and faces shaped by the pockmarked rock *are alive* and peering out intently from every crevice and cave."

Lake Superior, at the highest point of the Great Lakes, is the largest, cleanest, and least populated of the five lakes. Cape Gargantua is located in the heart of Lake Superior Provincial Park, a park that encompasses seventy-five miles of coastline. It's a wild and remote country—paddlers with keen eyes might spy moose, black bear, or wolves along the shore, or the elusive peregrines, which have made a comeback and populate Lake Superior's shoreline cliffs. A caution that every paddler needs to heed, even in summer, is that the open water is frigid, hovering in the low forties. If you go, you should seek out pockets of warm water in sheltered bays. These form the treasured, but elusive, Lake Superior swimming pools. "The Lake's cold water creates another bonus," Joanie continued, "an arctic microclimate where species like Arctic saxifrage and crowberry flourish. And other plants like orange lichens and purple bellflowers color Gargantua's shoreline particularly brilliantly at sunset."

OPPOSITE:
The islands of Cape Gargantua have long held deep spiritual significance for the Anishinaabe people.

DESTINATION

33

For the paddler and hiker, there are many routes throughout Lake Superior Provincial Park, ranging from day hikes to weeklong paddling excursions. "One thing I love about paddling at Gargantua is the Warp Bay beach and the coastal hiking trail," Joanie advises. "If the wind comes up, and you are obliged to stay onshore, there's so much you can do on the land."

One of Joanie's favorite memories of Gargantua concerns a moonlight paddle to Nanabijou's Chair. "This great rocky throne lies off Gargantua's northern extremity," she described. "In low waters, reefs reveal themselves in spidery threads reaching westwards from this monolith. The park's commonly used name, 'Devil's Chair,' was the product of overzealous missionaries eager to vanquish the Anishinaabe people's most powerful spiritual allies. But the stories of Nanabijou, the trickster who rested here after leaping across Lake Superior from his home in Thunder Bay, are being revived, as are the traditional ceremonies that have long been performed in this special landscape.

"On this occasion, we paddled from the beach at Warp Bay to Nanabijou's Chair at night, accompanied by a few friends. The lake was so calm and the stars so brightly reflected in the lake, it appeared as if we were floating in the middle of the universe. We took our deerskin drums with us. We lit a fire and warmed them until they were taut. And then we began drumming. With the deep primitive sound reverberating off the rock wall, drifting off into the night, we felt it could've been a thousand years ago. As I think back on that night, I can't help but conclude that our technology world of GPS's, cell phones, and laptops often distance us from these real-life experiences. Superior's first-hand teachings about respect for cold water, winds, and weather can never really be learned virtually. Knowing how and when to travel, that's important knowledge on Lake Superior. It is a commonality we share with all the people who have ever paddled here.

"People talk too much," Joanie laughed, "myself included. Speaking out to the night with our drums, not talking with words, trains us to listen more. The whole lake is speaking to us in the sound the water makes against shore. The animals, the birds, the insects, the trees; everything is speaking if we just take time to listen."

JOANIE MCGUFFIN and her husband, Gary, are wilderness adventurers, nature photographers, writers, and conservationists. They have canoed on waterways throughout North America, bicycled from the Arctic to the Pacific to the Atlantic oceans, backpacked the Appalachian Trail end to end, and sea-kayaked Greenland's fjords and

Mexico's Baja Peninsula. Between adventures, the McGuffins are ambassadors of the wilderness, touring with photo exhibitions and slide shows of their travels. Their eight published books include *Superior: Journeys on an Inland Sea* (a Great Lakes Book Award winner); *Paddle Your Own Canoe: An Illustrated Guide to the Art of Canoeing*; *Paddle Your Own Kayak*; *Where Rivers Run*; *In the Footsteps of Grey Owl: Journey Into the Ancient Forest*; *Great Lakes Journey: Exploring the Heritage Coast*; and *Quetico: Into the Wild*. They are currently working on establishing the Lake Superior Water Trail with Trans Canada Trail and the Lake Superior Watershed Conservancy (LSWC). Also with LSWC, they are working on a basinwide initiative for a Heritage Coast designation that recognizes the singular importance of this vast body of freshwater for the future of all who live within the Great Lakes watershed.

If You Go

▶ **Getting There:** Visitors to Gargantua generally fly into Sault Sainte Marie, Michigan/Ontario, which is served by several carriers, including Air Canada (888-247-2262; www.aircanada.com) and Delta (800-221-1212; www.delta.com). From here, it's roughly a hundred miles to Wawa, Ontario.

▶ **Best Time to Visit:** Longer camping trips are generally done in July and August.

▶ **Guides/Outfitters:** Several outfitters lead trips in the Superior Provincial Park area, including Naturally Superior Adventures (800-203-9092; www.naturallysuperior.com) and Caribou Expeditions (800-970-6662; www.caribou-expeditions.com).

▶ **Level of Experience:** Paddlers should have intermediate skills.

▶ **Accommodations:** Rock Island Lodge (800-203-9092; www.rockislandlodge.ca) and Voyageurs Lodge (877-877-7385; www.voyageurslodge.com) both offer on-the-lake lodging before and after your trip embarks.

DESTINATION

33

OTTAWA RIVER

RECOMMENDED BY **Jim Coffey**

"I like to describe the Ottawa as 'big bubbles, few troubles,'" said paddler Jim Coffey. "There's big white water for sure, but the river's drop-pool style makes it easy to recover if you flip a raft or someone swims. There aren't a lot of rocks or other hazards. Depending on the lines you choose, the Ottawa is ideal for both entry-level paddlers and white-water ninjas. In addition to its incredible rapids, the Ottawa has great accessibility. It's only sixty miles from the capital of Canada. In some places, when you're sixty miles outside the capital, it seems you're still *in the capital*. That's not the case on the Ottawa. You're out in a pristine wilderness region. You'll see ospreys and deer and pass a great blue heron rookery. People come to Canada to experience the wilderness. They might go to Niagara Falls; the waterfall is great, but it's surrounded by casinos and wax museums. It doesn't deliver on the image of Canada people have before visiting. The Ottawa does."

The Ottawa River flows nearly eight hundred miles from its headwaters in the Laurentian Mountains of central Quebec to its confluence with the St. Lawrence near Montreal. For much of its course, it defines the boundary between the province of Ontario and Quebec. As far as the paddling community is concerned, it's the eight-mile section around the Rocher Fendu islands (near the town of Davidson) that garners the greatest attention. Here, below McCoy's Chute, the river divides into two channels—the Middle and the Main—and flows warm and clear in a series of chutes, waves, and waterfalls that's been called eastern North America's Grand Canyon. The water is very clean and very warm, which adds to its appeal. "The channels are very distinct," Jim continued. "The Middle is a bit more technical in terms of the moves required; the Main has bigger waves. Most companies run one channel or the other. When I first started operating on the Ottawa, I thought it would be possible to run both in the same day. For me, doing one

OPPOSITE:
Warm water
and big rapids—
with a lack
of dangerous
obstacles—
make the Ottawa
a singular white-
water experience.

DESTINATION

34

without the other is like having French fries without vinegar or ketchup. So we run them both. Another nice thing about the Ottawa is that it's always runnable. Whether it has bigger water in the spring or lower flows in late summer, it's still very navigable . . . though it's quite a different river. I like to run it in smaller fourteen-foot rafts, which accentuate the intensity of the white water." Jim prefers to run the Middle Channel in the morning and Main after lunch. He described a few of the Ottawa's signature rapids.

"On the Middle Channel, Garvin's Chute is the standout. Essentially, Garvin's is a five-meter waterfall with four different drops, moving left to right: Staircase, ST Chute, Dragon's Tongue, and Elevator Shaft. It's a Class V, whatever amount of water is running and whichever drop you choose. When people see Garvin's, they often remark, 'It looks like it drops twenty feet!' That's because it does. Traditionally, rafters would run it on the left side, but we helped open up the right, which has steeper chutes.

"In the afternoon, we run the Main Channel, and the first rapid is one of the best—Lorne. Lorne is famous for its surfing waves, which draw kayakers from around the world. You ease into Lorne through some Class II+ rapids. When you drop into the first trough, there's a twenty-foot wave waiting. Our fourteen-foot boats fit on the wave; the front end hardly gets up to the peak. At the bottom, there's 'Bus Eater'—a huge hole you want to avoid. Before we enter Lorne, I tell people that we have a 50/50 chance of making it through without a spill. They can walk around if they wish, though, like most of the other rapids on the Ottawa, there are no hazards below, just fast, smooth water. You don't have to be conservative. If this was the first rapid you encountered, you might not want to do it. But as we've had a morning on the water already, they've built up to it, and most people go for the gusto.

"If there's one rapid that always comes up when people talk about the Ottawa, it's Coliseum. Coliseum has three giant house-size, roller-coaster-style waves. You go crashing through these fifteen- to twenty-foot waves. If you go in the water, you just swim to the right side, where there's a big pool. By the time they've made it through Coliseum, people who started the day as a newbie feel like they're ninjas. Paddle rafting builds that sort of confidence and sense of accomplishment. You know that no matter how good the guide, you won't get there without everyone working together. People leave feeling that they're ready for bigger challenges."

Rapids are often the sizzle that entices people to take river trips. Yet most people come away with a larger connection. Jim sees making that connection a big part of his job. "As guides, we're like alchemists. We need to turn a rafting trip—which some people almost view as a theme park ride—into something larger, an entire river experience. We have to interpret the natural and cultural history of the place. Some people see rivers like the Ottawa as a resource that needs to be harnessed. We can help them make the larger connection, to give the river, which can't speak for itself, a voice."

JIM COFFEY has worked in the white-water industry for over thirty years. He has competed on both a national and international level. Racing led to working as a white-water rafting guide, affording time and a place to train near world-class white water. This prompted a move to the Ottawa River valley, where he eventually founded Esprit Whitewater Worldwide. Jim captained the Canadian Rafting team to five top-ten finishes at the World Rafting Championships. He has worked on many of the world's greatest rivers in Canada, the United States, Mexico, Costa Rica, Chile, Argentina, Zambia, Zimbabwe, Italy, Australia, New Zealand, Indonesia, India, and Nepal. Through Esprit, he oversees rafting, canoeing, and kayaking operations in Canada, Mexico, and Costa Rica. In 1992, Jim started teaching classes for Rescue 3 in Eastern Canada and in 2010 started a strategic alliance with Raven Rescue as a specialist in providing training courses for the recreational and professional paddle sports industry.

If You Go

▶ **Getting There:** Most visitors will fly into Ottawa City, which is served by a number of carriers, including American Airlines (800-433-7300; www.aa.com) and Air Canada (800-776-3000; www.aircanada.com).

▶ **Best Time to Visit:** Rafters run the Ottawa from late April to mid-October. There's more water in the spring, less in the late summer, though the river always runs well.

▶ **Guides/Outfitters:** Esprit Whitewater Worldwide (800-596-7238; www.whitewater.ca) runs both channels in one day.

▶ **Level of Difficulty:** Beginner paddlers will do fine with a guide; nonguided rafters will need extensive Class IV/V experience.

▶ **Accommodations:** Esprit offers lodging near the river put-in at The Pointe. Ottawa Tourism (800-363-4465; www.ottawatourism.ca) lists a host of lodging options.

DESTINATION

34

HELLS CANYON

RECOMMENDED BY **Paul Arentsen**

There's a Nez Perce legend that claims that Hells Canyon—North America's deepest river gorge at nearly eight thousand feet—was dug by Coyote with a big stick to protect ancestors in Oregon's Blue Mountains from the Seven Devils (a mountain range of seven peaks) across the gorge in what is now Idaho. Geologists have a somewhat different explanation of the gorge's provenance. Either way, its grandeur is undeniable.

"The scale of the canyon was the thing that first struck me," said Paul Arentsen. "I grew up in Kentucky and had guided on some other big western rivers, but on my first float through Hells Canyon, I felt so small and insignificant. You also have the sheer power of the river. At the beginning of the rafting season in June you might have the river running at 35,000 CFS (cubic feet per second). [For comparison's sake: The maximum average discharge of the Colorado River at Lee's Ferry occurs in June, and is 32,500 CFS.] I remember lining up my fourteen-foot raft above the Wild Sheep Rapid the first time I ran the river and watching an eighteen-foot raft completely disappear in the waves in front of me. In addition to the hydrologic power and the size of the canyon, there's a rich cultural history in Hells Canyon: archeological evidence suggests at least twelve thousand years of human habitation. One of my guides was leading a group of teenagers down the river a few years back. As he was walking them to a wall that has pictographs, he was talking about the artifacts that are sometimes uncovered, like arrowheads. One boy interrupted him and held up an arrowhead. 'Like this?' he asked. It was right there on the trail. That gives you a sense of the layers of history here."

Hells Canyon is a loosely defined portion of the Snake River, the largest tributary of the mighty Columbia River. (There's some disagreement about where it begins and ends.) The 652,488-acre Hells Canyon National Recreation Area, which encompasses a

71-mile stretch of the Snake River, rests along the northern section of the Idaho-Oregon border. For paddling purposes, Hells Canyon begins below Hells Canyon Dam, where most rafters put in. There are two sections that are generally run—the 31-mile "Wild and Scenic" section to Pittsburg Landing or the longer 67-mile float to the take-out at mile 180. (Several other take-outs are available in between.) Whichever you choose, you're not long into the float before you reach Wild Sheep Rapid, one of the two biggest rapids on the river. Though the waves are sizable, a quick scout from the left side of the river will show seasoned rafters the proper line. The next big challenge is Granite Creek Rapids. "When you scout Granite Creek, it puts a pit in your belly," Paul continued. "There's a spot in the rapid called the Green Room that's the most exciting line. You need to have flows of at least 17,000 CFS to run it safely. It seems like the flows are always on the edge of 17K. We say that the Green Room is either open or closed. If it's open, you'll never forget it. You drop into this huge hole, and you're surrounded by waves—that's the Green Room. You think you're going to get pummeled, but there are times you won't even get a drop of water in the boat. I still vividly recall the first time I ran it. I was all charged up for the next two days."

After Granite Creek the rapids diminish in severity, but the scenery continues to improve, and there's more time for hikes and other activities. The canyon's vast elevation changes and mix of forests and grassland—not to mention its general isolation from humans—provide a tremendous habitat for a host of animals, including bighorn sheep, mountain goats, elk, and black bear. Bald eagles, golden eagles, and otters also call the canyon home. Hikes up the canyon will expose remnants of turn-of-the-century home-steader cabins and Native American relics like pit houses, rock shelters, and pictograph sites. "One of my favorite hikes is up Sheep Creek," Paul shared. "There's a nice trail up to an old homestead, and the creek has a pretty little swimming hole. Another hike people enjoy is near Pittsburg Landing, near the bottom of the Wild and Scenic section. You take switchbacks up a grassy slope until you've gained 1,500 or 2,000 feet of elevation. From here you can take in the full depth of the canyon. You also have a brilliant view of the Seven Devils."

Several sections of the Upper Snake River are renowned for their fishing. The Hells Canyon section may not get as much acclaim as these waters, though it's a fine stretch of water for *catching*. "It seems that every trip we have a boy or girl who's around twelve, and they're really eager to fish," Paul said. "I remember a pretrip meeting last year. A boy

DESTINATION

35

came in and all he could ask about was fishing. His dad was rolling his eyes. He set the goal of catching five fish by the end of the trip. He'd caught more than five smallmouth bass by the end of day one. He raised his quota to fifty by the end of day three. He beat that by the end of day two. That's a typical experience out here." In addition to bass, anglers will find rainbow trout, catfish, and white sturgeon—a prehistoric leviathan, clad in armorlike scales and reaching lengths that can eclipse ten feet.

"We fish for sturgeon almost every trip," Paul added. "When hooked, they'll tail-walk and jump—it really freaks people out. One place we fish for them is called Sturgeon Rock, so named because settlers used to hang sturgeon they'd caught off iron bolts attached to the rock and sell them to passing paddle wheelers. I love watching a kid reel in a 250-pound sturgeon. They want to give up, but we encourage them to stay at it. Once we land the fish, we roll it over on its back in the water so the lucky fisherman can give it a big kiss on the mouth before we let it go."

OPPOSITE:
A comfortable camp in the Hells Canyon section of the Snake River—America's deepest river gorge.

PAUL ARENTSEN met his wife, Penny Rieken, in the Wallowa Mountains back in 1997 while leading wilderness outdoor education trips. They formed Winding Waters River Expeditions soon after. Rafting guide Morgan Jenkins soon joined them. Today, they guide the Lower Salmon, Grande Ronde, and Hells Canyon section of the Snake.

If You Go

▶ **Getting There:** The towns of Joseph and Halfway in Oregon are the jumping-off points for Hells Canyon adventures. They're each roughly six hours east of Portland.

▶ **Best Time to Visit:** Guided trips are led June through August.

▶ **Guides/Outfitters:** Several outfitters lead trips through Hells Canyon, including Winding Waters River Expeditions (877-426-7238; www.windingwatersrafting.com).

▶ **Level of Difficulty:** Paddlers on a guided trip don't need any previous experience; do-it-yourselfers will need Class IV skills to run Granite Creek and Wild Sheep Rapids.

▶ **Accommodations:** Trips begin and end in Joseph. The Joseph Chamber of Commerce (800-585-4121; www.josephoregon.com) can help with lodging.

DESTINATION

35

ROGUE RIVER

RECOMMENDED BY **Brad Niva**

The Rogue may not be the longest or wildest float among the West's iconic rafting rivers. Yet it has a number of features that make it a perennial favorite for many paddlers.

"Most would agree that the Rogue is the crown jewel of Oregon," Brad Niva began. "It's one of the few western rivers that people regularly run that goes right to the Pacific. Many of the popular rivers are in high desert canyon country. The Rogue cuts right through the Siskiyou Mountains, past big old-growth Douglas fir as well as dense deciduous forests. The area is lush, and the environs support a large number of animals—black bears, great blue herons, bald eagles, elk, and otters—and there's a chance you could see these creatures any day you're out there. You're very much in the wilderness, but the Rogue is extremely accessible; it starts within twenty-five miles of Interstate 5 and ends within twenty-six miles of Highway 101. It's a fairly short float, roughly forty miles, so visitors can have a great river experience over three or four days."

The Rogue rises near Crater Lake in Oregon's Cascade Mountains and flows 215 miles in a generally westerly direction, crossing the relatively populated regions of Medford and Grants Pass before reaching the Siskiyous and finally entering the Pacific at the town of Gold Beach. The river gained some notoriety in the 1920s from western novelist Zane Grey, who loved the Rogue for its steelhead and salmon fishing, and frequently wrote of it in the outdoors magazines of the day. The resulting influx of tourists created an early and vibrant river-guiding culture. One of the early guides, Glen Wooldridge would float clients from Grants Pass to Gold Beach, eating what he and his clients could catch and shoot and camping along the way.

Remnants of the Rogue's rich history can be experienced firsthand. These include Whisky Creek Cabin, built by an unknown miner in 1880, and the Zane Grey Cabin near

OPPOSITE:
Brad Niva
describes Mule
Creek Canyon as
"the closest thing
to a Disneyland
ride in Mother
Nature."

Winkle Bar, where he spent many autumns writing and fishing for steelhead. Both are on the National Register of Historic Places.

Though there are boating opportunities on many stretches of the Rogue, the main section of interest to paddlers is the thirty-four-mile run between Galice and Agness. This portion of the river was part of the first portion of the Rogue that was protected by the National Wild and Scenic Rivers Act. "I feel that the Rogue gives rafters beautiful scenery with just enough rapids to give you a dose of adrenaline, without anything too extreme," Brad continued. "Thanks to the nature of the river and its relatively short length, it's a perfect entry point for new wilderness paddlers."

Another aspect of the Rogue that makes it amenable to new rafters—or, for that matter, to seasoned and *comfort-minded* rafters—is the sprinkling of rustic lodges interspersed along the Wild and Scenic section of the river. "Every river has camping," Brad added. "But on how many rivers can you go from lodge to lodge . . . or mix a few nights of camping with a stay at a lodge?" There are three lodges altogether: Black Bar, Marial, and Paradise. "Each one has its own charms and personality," Brad continued, "but all are clean and comfortable and A-1 in hospitality . . . and off the grid, so you're not tempted to check your e-mail or make a phone call. If you're on the river earlier in the season when it's chilly or get caught in a downpour, you're so glad you don't have to climb into a tent. Each lodge has its food specialty. Black Bar is famous for its fried chicken. Marial is known for its homemade biscuits served with blackberry jam. Paradise features all-you-can-eat ribs and chicken served with garlic mashed potatoes.

Though perhaps not as daunting as the rapids on the Colorado, the Rogue has several stretches that will bring out a paddler's best game. Brad described the river's "Big Three." "First, you have Rainie Falls, which is the only Class V on the river. Back in the day, it was considered impassable. With the help of a little dynamite, it's now more runnable. You have three options to run Rainie. The first is to go right over the main falls, which have anywhere from an eight-foot to twelve-foot drop. This is doable, but not recommended. The second is the Middle Chute, which is challenging but possible for a seasoned rafter. The third and most tried-and-true route is down the fish ladder, which is recommended for the occasional rafter. Mule Creek Canyon, a Class IV, is next. Here, the whole river pinches down to a width of seventeen feet, sandwiched between deep basalt walls. This is the closest thing to a Disneyland ride in Mother Nature. The stretch is full of seams and boils, and you can get pinched up against the walls. I make sure everybody has their hands and feet in the boat and just let it bounce along.

"On every big river, there's one spot that gives you butterflies. On the Rogue, that spot is Class IV Blossom Bar. When you stop to scout it, this rock garden doesn't look like that much. But the power of the water here is massive, and if you make a mistake, there can be consequences. [Five rafters, all on private trips, have perished here since 2007.] Blossom Bar is very technical; there are three moves you need to make. If you miss any of these steps, odds are good you'll be stuck on the Picket Fence section (a series of jagged rocks) for the afternoon."

There's an easy-to-access trail for guests who'd prefer to walk around Blossom Bar.

BRAD NIVA became interested in white-water rafting while living in Bend, Oregon. He became obsessed with rivers and rafted throughout the west. In 1998, he took a trip on the Rogue with Rogue Wilderness Adventures (RWA). The river spoke to him in a special way. Some years later, the owner of RWA asked him in jest if he was ready to buy the company. He did it and has been operating the company since 2006.

If You Go

▶ **Getting There:** Guests can fly into Portland and drive four hours south or fly into Medford, which is served by several carriers, including Horizon (800-252-7522; www.horizonair.com) and United Express (800-241-6522; www.united.com).

▶ **Best Time to Visit:** The season runs May through September.

▶ **Guides/Outfitters:** A number of companies lead trips on the Rogue, including Rogue Wilderness Adventures (800-336-1647; www.wildrogue.com).

▶ **Level of Difficulty:** The Rogue is rated Class III, though there are several Class IV rapids. Do-it-yourselfers should be advanced paddlers; beginners will be fine on guided trips.

▶ **Accommodations:** Rogue Wilderness Adventures lists a number of lodging options for the night before the trip on its website (www.wildrogue.com).

SAN BLAS ARCHIPELAGO

RECOMMENDED BY **Javier Romero Gerbaud**

The islands of the San Blas Archipelago have a singular appeal: They allow visitors to simultaneously experience an ancient (and mostly intact) culture along with an unspoiled and barely discovered Caribbean paradise. As the *New York Times* put it in 2008, the San Blas are "one of the few vacation spots that both an anthropologist and a beach bum can agree on."

"The San Blas are part of Guna Yala, and Guna Yala is a country within a country," Javier Romero Gerbaud described. "The Guna people are Panamanian, but they are also a people unto themselves, committed to the old ways. There are some elements of modernity here, but overall, development has been very slow. The Gunas are very wise people. They understand that they have a gem and are not going to ruin it. They will develop it at their own pace, not give it away to a foreign investor for a quick return. I've had some poorly informed guests come to the San Blas, and within an hour, they want to go back to the mainland. Why? There's no luxury. No air-conditioning. No Jet Skis or other toys on the beach, no fast food. It's hard to get a cold drink. In that respect, it's not for everyone. Though if you want that sort of experience, you can go to Cancun."

The San Blas Islands rest just off the north coast of Panama, east of the Panama Canal. The roughly 365 coral islands that make up the San Blas extend one hundred miles from Puerto Obaldia in the southeast to El Porvenir in the northwest and make up part of the semi-autonomous territory Guna Yala. Less than fifty of the islands are inhabited, some by only a handful of families. The Guna (sometimes called Kuna) people settled the islands of the archipelago in the first half of the sixteenth century after fleeing subjugation under the Spanish colonialists and continued their largely subsistence lifestyle as existence on the mainland came under the sway of European influence. Four hundred

OPPOSITE:
The San Blas offers paddlers exposure to a Caribbean removed from modern influences.

DESTINATION

37

years later, the Guna way of life faced suppression again, this time from the Panamanian government. In 1925, they rebelled against policies banning traditional dress and spiritual customs and were eventually granted special status. (A portion of the semi-autonomous region, or *comarca*, resides in the Darien region of the mainland.)

Thanks to the controls the Guna people have placed upon the San Blas, accommodating tourists is a relatively new development. Javier described how he came to begin leading paddling tours. "Aventuras Panama was originally a rafting company. A few years back, I met a Canadian who wanted to bring guests to the San Blas, and we got together to try to make it happen. I worked with several of the local *Sailas* (chiefs) to obtain permission, and it was granted. I remember getting into a dugout canoe outfitted with a motor after getting off the plane. As we were heading to our first island, six dolphins came up along the canoe. We put on our masks and jumped in with them; they weren't more than twelve feet away. Each time I tried to reach out and touch them, they'd pull back, but when I'd swim toward the boat, they'd swim close to check me out. It was a nice greeting."

There are several options for exploring the San Blas by kayak. Some outfitters will break camp each day and move from island to island. Javier prefers a more relaxed pace, setting up a base camp and doing day paddles. "We make arrangements to stay at an island that has at least one family residing on it and that is not too far from other islands, so it's possible to paddle there and back. The families rely mostly on fishing and coconuts to sustain themselves. Coconuts have historically been a form of currency for the Guna, and they're still swapped for oil and canned food. We have a support boat that brings out supplies, tents, and water. (Some of the islands have wells, but the water isn't potable.) Each day, we paddle to a different island. Some may have five families living there, others fifteen. We avoid the bigger settlements." Each day allows plenty of time for snorkeling along the islands' pristine reefs, considered the best Panama has to offer. Dolphins, sea turtles, rays, and a host of reef fish await.

One of the most unique aspects of Guna culture is its bright-colored clothing—especially the *mola*. Molas consist of layers of fabric intricately cut and sewn together by Guna women, depicting traditional geometric designs, and more recently, scenes from the natural world. Originally, these designs were painted directly onto the body. As missionaries and government officials encouraged the Guna to wear clothing in the nineteenth century, the designs were incorporated into cloth that was in turn sewn into blouses, one in front, and one in back. (Both squares of cloth and the blouses are referred to as molas.) "The more layers to each mola, the more value it has," Javier explained. Guna women are readily identified by their gold nose rings. Infant girls have their noses pierced within four months of their birth as part of the Needle Festival (Ico-Inna); the ring will be worn for the remainder of their lives. Women also adorn their legs with loops of bright-colored beads.

Panama may not be on everyone's travel map yet, but Javier thinks that will change soon. "I like to compare Panama to Costa Rica," he ventured. "They are fifteen or twenty years ahead of us in terms of developing their ecotourism business, and it's certainly been discovered. In fact, in some places, you might have a problem finding a local person in Costa Rica. In Panama, it's all local people. We have all the natural features that Costa Rica has, except a live volcano, and a rich history—the pre-Colonial Indian culture and later the Spaniards. And we also have three indigenous cultures, each a wonderful attraction in itself. Not to mention the Panama Canal."

JAVIER ROMERO GERBAUD is a native Panamanian. Educated at Purdue University, he started Aventuras Panama in 1994. Javier's company—the first adventure-oriented outfitter in Panama—regularly leads trips to Chagres National Park, the Mamoni River, the Rio Grande, the Chiriqui River, the Embera River, and Guna Yala.

If You Go

▶ **Getting There:** Trips begin and end in Panama City, which is served by a number of carriers, including American Airlines (800-433-7300; www.aa.com) and Copa Airlines (800-359-2672; www.copaair.com).

▶ **Best Time to Visit:** Though temperatures are clement year-round, wind conditions are most favorable to kayaking from November through March.

▶ **Guides/Outfitters:** Several companies lead excursions in the San Blas, including Aventuras Panama (800-614-7214; www.aventuraspanama.com) and Southern Sea Ventures (+61 2 8901 3287; www.southernseaventures.com).

▶ **Level of Difficulty:** This trip is best suited for paddlers of at least intermediate ability.

▶ **Accommodations:** Visit Panama (www.visitpanama.com) lists lodging options in Panama City; your outfitter will likely have a preferred hotel property.

TAMBOPATA RIVER

RECOMMENDED BY **Ken Johnson**

When asked about one of his favorite river trips, seasoned guide Ken Johnson paused. "The Tambopata is one of the most special rivers I've ever floated," he began. "Though at the same time, it's not a river trip I would necessarily recommend to anyone else. It's very hard to get there. You're going to have a level of discomfort. You'll be hard-pressed to find anyone else who's been there to help with logistics. It's impossible to get any idea of what the flows are going to be at any given time, and once you're at the put-in, you're pretty much committed."

So why endure discomfort and even danger to float this Peruvian drainage? Floating the Tambopata takes you through the heart of one of the most biodiverse regions in the world . . . and you can be all but assured that you will see no other humans beyond your party for the six days you're on the river.

The Tambopata is a river, a reserve, and a province in the Madre de Dios state of southeastern Peru, in the heart of Peruvian Amazonia. The river flows in a northerly direction, beginning northeast of Lake Titicaca (the highest navigable lake in the world, at an elevation over 12,500 feet) and joining the Madre de Dios River near the city of Puerto Maldonado, roughly 35 miles from the Bolivian border. The Tambopata National Reserve encompasses a million acres of rainforests and tropical savannahs. The forests—including vast tracts of old-growth ceibas reaching over ninety feet—are virtually impenetrable; the region can only be accessed by water. Though the reserve has been only lightly explored, a vast number of animal species have been recorded, including over 670 bird species.

"I've done a lot of rafting in Central and South America and have many contacts in the region," Ken continued. "A group of Venturer Scouts from Iowa contacted me to see if I could help them set up a special trip that was in Latin America, tropical, and completely off the grid. I made a few calls and the Tambopata came up among several options. One of my outfitter friends in Cuzco had run it and figured out the logistics of doing so. Just as important, he assembled an elite crew of guides from Argentina, Chile, and Peru who were game to lead my group. I made sure that the Venturer Scouts group was amenable to the uncertainty, challenge, and cost of mounting such an expedition, and they were. So we set a date to depart."

The meeting point was the Juliaca Airport, near Lake Titicaca. The first challenge sojourners face is acclimatizing to the elevation. The second is the drive to the put-in. "This is one of the more harrowing drives you'll ever take, anywhere," Ken continued. "It's hard to describe how bad the road is; it's actually been featured on a BBC program called *World's Most Dangerous Roads*. And the drive takes almost two days. As you crawl along, you have little sense of how far you're going to get or where you're going to sleep. The first night, we stayed in a small town at what passed for a hotel. The next day we reached the river."

One of Ken's concerns was quickly assuaged—there was enough water in the river, but not too much. A six-day, hundred-mile expedition began on what the few people who've run the upper Tambopata rank a Class III/Class IV river. "The upper section of the river was fairly technical, requiring a lot of moves to avoid hitting massive holes or wrapping around rocks," Ken continued. "A number of tributaries entered the river each day, effectively doubling the volume. As more water entered, the rowing became a bit easier— there were big roller-coaster waves but less complicated maneuvering. By the last few days, the river had grown quite large and was placid. We covered between fifteen and eighteen miles a day."

The challenge of the Tambopata's rapids is dwarfed by the sense of exploration this trip affords and the chance to be absorbed in one of Amazonia's most unspoiled places. "The jungle foliage was so thick, it was pretty much impossible to hike in at all," Ken recalled. "But even without leaving the river, we saw the most incredible birdlife. Every beach we stopped at had tracks or other evidence of jaguar. We didn't run into a single human being. After a layover day at the confluence with a major trib, we were met by a motorboat. It was a full day's ride down to the Tambopata Research Center. To put our isolation into perspective: Most people seeking a Peruvian wilderness experience take a motorboat *upstream* three hours to the research center.

"I carry a kaleidoscope of images in my head of that trip. But the most ineffable memories concern the group of guides we'd assembled. In the evening, they'd share anecdotes that weaved between where they'd been, both geographically and metaphysically. They weren't bragging, but they'd had some amazing experiences. I doubt you could ever replicate this group of river people."

KEN JOHNSON grew up traveling around the country and the world. His travel résumé includes venturing across the United States on freight trains, trekking in Nepal, kayaking in Alaska, spearfishing in Bali, riding his bike across Cuba, and extensive travel throughout Latin America. In the mid-eighties, Ken worked to explore and map the rafting routes on Guatemala's rivers and actually got to name some of the rapids himself. In the summer of 2011, he organized and participated in a seven-day descent of Peru's Tambopata River. Ken currently works as a travel planner with eXito Travel, where he specializes in organizing family vacations, scientific research expeditions, and philanthropic missions in Latin America.

OPPOSITE:
The upper Tambopata, where the Andes meet Amazonia, is so far off the grid that you're virtually assured solitude.

If You Go

▶ **Getting There:** Intrepid visitors will travel to Lima, which is served by many carriers, and then on to Juliaca, which is served by LAN (866-435-9526; www.lan.com). The trip ends near Puerto Maldonado, which is also served by LAN.

▶ **Best Time to Visit:** Jungle temperatures are more reasonable (in the 70s and 80s) from June through August, the austral winter.

▶ **Guides/Outfitters:** Ken Johnson (800-655-4053, ext. 8531; ken@exitotravel.com) can help you arrange a Tambopata adventure. O.A.R.S (800-346-6277; www.oars.com) has recently begun leading trips that include a few days exploring Lake Titicaca in sea kayaks.

▶ **Level of Difficulty:** This is an adventure for only the hardiest white-water enthusiasts.

▶ **Accommodations:** Libertador Lake Titicaca (877-778-2281; www.libertador.com.pe) offers luxurious lodging for before you leave for the put-in; the float concludes a motorboat's ride away from Tambopata Research Center (www.tambopata.com).

DESTINATION

38

MAGPIE RIVER

RECOMMENDED BY **Eric Hertz**

"When I describe the wonders of the Magpie to people, they don't believe that it could be in Quebec," Eric Hertz began. "They find it hard to believe that there could be such an incredible wilderness river with scores of rapids and falls (nearly one hundred), wolves, bears, moose, caribou, and native brook trout—and few if any people—just five hundred miles northeast of Montreal. It's so isolated, the only way to get in is by floatplane. The water is so clean, you can actually drink right out of the river. And though the Magpie supports trout, the water is temperate. You don't need a wetsuit to run it, and it's quite comfortable to swim in its deep, clear pools.

"In terms of scenery, unspoiled wilderness, exceptional fishing, spectacular camps, and numerous Class IV rapids, the Magpie is without question one of the greatest white-water rafting destinations in the world. Seeing other people on the river is rare; in fact, the river is so rarely run that most of its rapids have never even been named."

The Magpie begins at Magpie Lake on the Labrador Plateau in far eastern Quebec and flows approximately 120 miles south until it reaches the Gulf of St. Lawrence. It rushes through a roadless boreal wilderness of dense pine and spruce forests and smooth granite banks, typical of the Canadian Shield. "The Magpie was the first river that we found after Earth Rivers was formed back in 1989," Eric continued. "First we located it on some topographical maps. Then we found someone who had canoed it. Finally we flew over it, and then floated it. We figured that if the Magpie was this good, there must be a dozen other rivers in eastern Quebec that would be equally worthwhile. We explored a few, the Romaine and the Moisie. They were not the Magpie.

"An aspect of the Magpie that I really like is the fact that it builds and builds. It's not much fun to be on a river trip where the climactic white water is at the beginning of the

OPPOSITE:

The Magpie may be the greatest white-water river you've never heard of.

DESTINATION

39

175

trip and there's flat water thereafter. The rapids get more plentiful and more intense as the trip unfolds, the scenery gets grander and grander, and even the camps keep improving." Bugs can be a problem in June and even July, but by August, they've largely abated, and paddlers are treated to warm, low-humidity days and pleasingly cool nights. At night, you can take in the pulsing light show of the aurora borealis.

The iconic animals of the boreal forest are seldom seen along the river, though moose, bear, and wolf tracks are often found in the sand around camps. On one occasion, however, Eric was privy to a special lupine display. "I was coming down a Class IV rapid with a group and I happened to glance over at a cliff that ran parallel to the river," he recalled. "There were these large dogs hopping from rock to rock—it suddenly clicked that they were wolves. The wind was blowing upstream at the time, so our scent was not reaching them. They moved toward the bottom of the rapid, still hopping from rock to rock, and they had no idea that we were coming near. We were only about fifty feet away before they noticed us. It was a unique experience to get that close to wolves."

Though most of the rapids and falls on the Magpie are unnamed, Eric and his team had an occasion to name one waterfall. "There's a thirteen-foot sliding waterfall with a curl at the bottom. It looks horrendous, but it's not terrible if you hit the right line. On this one trip, we had a guy rowing the baggage boat who was pretty self-confident. He was letting everyone know he thought the river was pretty easy. We would generally stop and scout the fall in question, but I had it memorized and knew just where to line up. Before we got there, the other guides and I planned that we wouldn't stop to scout. The falls came up suddenly, and as we approached, the guy on the baggage boat had his feet up on the oars—a casual attitude that he'd had most of the trip. My Earth River partner Robert dropped into the falls and disappeared, then me, and finally Dan, the other guide. We looked up and saw the new guy putting on his brakes, pulling like mad to avoid getting swept in. Once he scouted it and came down the falls, Dan asked him, 'How come you had to scout that one?' From then on, it was known as Trust Falls."

There's another named rapid on the Magpie that will never be run again. "A few years back, we were battling the planned damming of the Lower Magpie," Eric recalled. "The dam was going to eliminate a twenty-five-foot waterfall that some kayakers had dubbed Eternity Falls, as well as a Class V rock garden that was unnamed. As part of the effort to rally support, I took a boat full of prominent lawyers down the river. When we hit the rock garden the boat flipped, and we were all swimming. That's when the rapid got its name—Litigation Falls.

"We lost that battle, and the dam went in. Eternity Falls and Litigation Falls are covered, gone forever. But thankfully, only the last kilometer of the Magpie was impacted. As it is, it's just a scratch on a diamond."

ERIC HERTZ began guiding at sixteen and founded Earth Rivers in the late 1980s on the following principles: exploring and finding the most amazing trips; running the finest, safest trips possible; and fighting to preserve important river resources. Over the past twenty-three years, he has organized and led dozens of conservation-awareness trips, taking policy makers and media down threatened rivers. His efforts focused on stopping the James Bay hydroelectric project in Quebec and dams on Chile's Bìo-Bìo and Futaleufú Rivers and Quebec's Magpie. Eric's other conservation efforts helped bring awareness to the preservation of watersheds like British Columbia's Yosemite-like Headwall Canyon and Newfoundland's Main River, which were both threatened by clear-cut logging. Using his land trust experience, he and his partner, Robert Currie, founded the Earth River Land Trust on the Futaleufú, which to date has protected over twenty kilometers of the river's most dramatic shoreline. Eric was the trip leader and captained the lead boat on a number of notable first raft descents including the Futaleufú, Magpie, Headwall Canyon, and Tibet's Schulo.

If You Go

▶ **Getting There:** The staging area for Magpie floats is Sept-Îles, Quebec, which is served via Montreal by Air Canada (800-776-3000; www.aircanada.com).

▶ **Best Time to Visit:** August through mid-September. The river can be run earlier in the summer, but the black flies can be overwhelming.

▶ **Guides/Outfitters:** Earth River (800-643-2784; www.earthriver.com) pioneered commercial excursions on the Magpie.

▶ **Level of Difficulty:** Beginner paddlers are welcome on guided trips.

▶ **Accommodations:** Lodging for night seven in Sept-Îles is included in the Earth River tour.

DESTINATION

39

KAA-KHEM RIVER

RECOMMENDED BY **Vladimir Gavrilov**

"Though I'm a high school teacher in California during the year, I guide a number of trips on the Middle Fork of the Salmon in Idaho each July," Vladimir Gavrilov began. "When I try to describe one of my favorite rivers in my Russian homeland, the Kaa-Khem, to American friends, I say that it's Russia's version of the Middle Fork. It's a river of great clarity that flows through a pristine taiga wilderness with a brisk current. It's mountainous country, but the mountains are soft. And like the Middle Fork, Kaa-Khem has some memorable rapids and great fishing. I'm always struck by the air. It's the tastiest air I've ever experienced."

OPPOSITE:
Very few
foreigners have
ever paddled
the Kaa-Khem,
but it's gained a
following among
Russian paddlers.

Like Patagonia or Texas, Siberia is for many as much a state of mind as a place, an expression of banishment, isolation, and deprivation. The region's physical grandeur rivals its psychological weight; Siberia makes up over 75 percent of Russia's territory and the lion's share of north Asia, stretching from the Arctic Ocean in the north to Kazakhstan, Mongolia, and China to the south. The Kaa-Khem flows through the Sayan Mountains in south central Siberia, just north of the Mongolian border. Floats begin just 50 miles from Mongolia and terminate 160-odd miles to the north, not far beyond the Kaa-Khem's confluence with the Kyzyl Khem. En route, you pass through the Tuva Republic, perhaps best known for its musical export, Tuvan throat singers. "On this trip, you pass through the very center of the Asian subcontinent," Vladimir added. "You reach a point where you are as far away from an ocean as you can get in the world."

Russian rafters have known of the Kaa-Khem for a number of years; Vladimir first ran it in 1986, in the early days of Russian recreational river running. Yet its remote location has made it virtually unknown outside of Russia's borders. A lack of roads (or any other rafting infrastructure) makes getting to the Kaa-Khem at least as challenging as running

179

the rapids of the Mel'zeyskiy Cascade. "You can get there by helicopter, but it's very expensive—$25,000 for round-trip passage," Vladimir continued. "We get there using a six-wheeled Russian military truck. Half of the trip is off-road, and it takes two days to get in. The put-in is at a small Tuvan village called Kungurtuk. Once we begin our float, we're not likely to see any other people on the water."

There are certainly rivers in the Sayan that might have more appeal for adrenaline junkies, though through an eight-day float on the Kaa-Khem, you'll find your share of Class III/IV rapids. As alluded to earlier, the most challenging stretch is the Mel'zeyskiy Cascade, a section of river ten miles long containing more than thirty rapids that surge over granite bedrock. The Russians are an extremely resourceful, self-reliant people—because if things go wrong in Siberia, who can you call? This applies to raft repair. "On one trip, one of our cat rafts broke part of its frame after Rapid #19," Vladimir recalled. "One of our guides, Anatoli, found a piece of wood on the bank and created a brace to strengthen the frame. The brace worked for the entire trip." Another memorable set of rapids comes in a section of the river called The Cheeks—a Russian term for narrow gorges with high vertical walls. On the Kaa-Khem's Cheeks, ten rapids await.

While you're not likely to encounter any other recreationists on the river, you will come upon one habitation, Katazy Village, which was settled by a group of Old Believers. "Old Believers fled civilization because they didn't agree with the reforms Peter the Great made to the Russian Orthodox Church," Vladimir shared. "The settlement in Katazy Village has ten families, seventy people. Their only connections with the outside world are the very infrequent rafters and an occasional stop by a military helicopter that drops off fuel for their tractor and might take ill residents back to larger settlements for care. The men basically ignore you, but the women are more open. We always bring medicine for them, because it's in short supply. They have large gardens and keep some cows. We usually can buy some dairy products and vegetables from them."

Rafters who've become accustomed to elaborate camp kitchens and meals rivaling those served in Michelin-starred restaurants may be taken aback at first by the provisions on the Kaa-Khem—even with the help of the Old Believers. "We don't have access to big coolers or plentiful ice supplies, so we have to minimize fresh and frozen goods that we bring along," Vladimir explained. "Still, most guests enjoy our food, which is classically Russian. One Russian staple is sala, which is a cured meat, like bacon. Some foreigners make faces when I bring it out. But once they overcome their disgust and try it, they love it and want to know why they can't have more. We make pancakes for breakfast—Russian pancakes are the best in the world—and dinners include lots of soups, including borscht. We cook almost everything over a campfire. First thing we do when we stop for lunch or make camp is gather wood. On river trips in Russia, fire is always with you!"

The cold, clear waters of the Kaa-Khem can supplement your meals . . . with a little luck. Grayling and lenok (a member of the trout family) are present in good numbers. So are taimen, the world's largest salmonid, which can reach weights of over a hundred pounds. "On one of my trips, we caught a taimen on the first night of our trip. It was almost four feet long, and we ate it for three days. The head was so big, we couldn't fit it into the pot to make fish soup."

VLADIMIR GAVRILOV earned two PhDs in solid-state physics and published more than a hundred scientific articles and one book while living in the former Soviet Union. Much of his free time was spent leading expeditions on all types of rivers in Russia and especially Siberia. His love for rivers brought him to a rafting competition in Costa Rica, where he was recruited to guide on the Class IV Tuolumne River in California. In 1991, his guiding skills allowed him to move to California and bring his family there two years later. He now works as a river guide in the summer for Echo River Trips and as an AP Physics teacher during the off season. His book *Rivers of an Unknown Land*, about the rivers of the former Soviet Union, was published in 2004.

If You Go

▶ **Getting There:** You can reach Abakan, Kaa-Khem's staging point, from Moscow on Aeroflot (+86-687-97647; www.aeroflot.ru). From here, it's still a two-day drive to the put-in.
▶ **Best Time to Visit:** The season is brief—most run the Kaa-Khem in July or August.
▶ **Guides/Outfitters:** Echo River Trips (800-652-3246; www.echotrips.com) arranges and leads trips on the Kaa-Khem and handles lodging on either end of the trip.
▶ **Level of Difficulty:** Given the logistical challenges of running trips on Siberian rivers, this trip is not advised for do-it-yourselfers . . . or novices.

THE SHETLAND ISLANDS

RECOMMENDED BY **Angus Nicol**

Few regions of the world deliver on the promise of "rugged beauty" as eloquently and definitively as the Shetland Islands. The Shetland Islands are the northernmost archipelago in the United Kingdom, part of the Crown's domain, yet a land unto itself, breaching the Atlantic and the North Atlantic. (London is nearly twice as distant as the coast of Norway; it's no wonder that Shetlanders feel a certain affinity for the Vikings.)

OPPOSITE:
An exceptionally
calm day on the
north side of
Muckle Roe—
a favorite of
paddlers on the
Shetland Islands.

"Our coastline is extremely exposed," Angus Nicol explained. "There's nothing between the Shetland Islands and North America, and the waves can really build. Over time, they've carved the cliffs into wonderful shapes—magnificent caves, arches, pillars, and sea stacks. On top of that, you've got a tremendous diversity of rock—granite, limestone, and sandstone. The Shetland Islands are like a geology park. To explore the exposed shorelines by kayak, you need to have good conditions, which you're most likely to see in the summer. But the inland waters offer a more sheltered setting for paddling, even in the winter. There's a great deal of history around the islands, though some of the relics require a bit of explanation from someone with local knowledge. There's some incredible birdlife here, and you have the chance of meeting dolphins, otters, and whales."

The Shetland Islands comprise over one hundred islands that begin roughly one hundred miles north of the Scottish mainland and stretch another hundred miles north. Only fifteen of the islands are inhabited, with most of the 22,000 souls that call this hardy land home living on the largest island, which is simply called Mainland. Archeologists believe that the Shetland Islands were inhabited as early as 4000 BC; Vikings arrived from Norway around AD 800 and colonized the islands soon after. (As most structures were built of stone, many exist to this day in varied states of disrepair.) Norway would rule the Shetland Islands until the late fifteenth century, when the islands were ceded to Scotland.

Fishing has always been an important part of the Shetland economy and still exceeds income generated from offshore oil production. Sheep are also still raised here to provide the wool for their namesake sweaters, among other uses.

There's nearly 1,700 miles of coastline to explore around the Shetland Islands. Angus will choose a day's adventure depending on the weather. "It doesn't take long to drive from one area to another," he continued, "and we'll choose different spots as the wind permits. If weather is good and the tide swells are not too bad, you can take an absolute beginner to amazing coastline and be safe. But if you make silly or careless decisions, the sea is not forgiving." One favorite spot to visit is Muckle Roe, a small island just off the west coast of Mainland on St. Magnus Bay. It takes its name from the red granite that makes up its substrate, and its coastline is riddled with caves, stacks, and arches. "On a good-weather day, it's easy to navigate the south end of the island," Angus added. "On a very good day, you can paddle all the way around. Muckle Roe has some very friendly caves that inexperienced kayakers can explore, as there's no surge to speak of. Some caves are only as wide as your boat; some are massive. There are spots where you can link a few caves together and come back out on the water a ways down from where you started, which is always special. Once your eyes get adjusted to the light in the cave, you can see down quite far. The water is very deep."

Papa Stour, also on St. Magnus Bay, is another favorite spot for Angus. "Papa Stour is famous for the character of its caves, which are packed into a small area," he continued. "It's absolutely magnificent, but not as good for beginners. There are some strong tides around it, and you need to have three settled days on the Atlantic for it to be settled enough to go in close . . . and for me, there's no sense in paddling if you can't go in close. A day on the water at Papa Stour begins with a twenty-minute passage across the Sound of Papa from Mainland; ideally you'll have slack tides. If you head in a northwesterly direction, you'll come to Kirstan's Hole, a spectacular cave that has a natural skylight because its top fell in. A little farther up the coast, there are some small islands seaward. The innermost island has a network of north-south passages. There's a high stack just to the south. It's absolutely charming, though even on a calm day, there's some surge and lift.

"A little farther along and you reach Hole of Boardie [sometimes called Boardie Tunnel]. It's one of the world's longest sea passages at nearly four hundred meters. The tide runs through it, and you need very good conditions to enter. You find yourself paddling in the darkness with a headlamp, but there's a glow from the end. At the north end, there is a network of beautiful arches and stacks to pass through. The sunlight seems to dance as it sparkles through the rocks. To me, it's prettier than the long tunnels. As you begin to head south, you pass more caves. Near where the ferry comes in from Mainland, there's a rock called Maiden Stack. One story goes that a nobleman built a tiny house at the top of the stack, where he kept his daughter to keep her away from her lover. [In one version of the story, when she was allowed to leave, she was pregnant; the ruins of the house are still visible.] Maiden Stack is riddled with passages; it's more caves than rock, and there's wonderful light coming through. By the time you've come through, you're back at the south end of Papa Stour."

The island of Unst is the northernmost inhabited landmass in the United Kingdom, and the cliffs of Hermaness are on the northernmost point on the island. The cliffs have been designated a national nature reserve, as it's a breeding ground for many birds. "One day my wife and I were paddling past Hermaness," Angus recalled, "and the sky above us erupted with a multitude of gannets swooping off the cliffs, diving all around us. There were flocks and flocks of gannets. The noise of them took our breath away."

ANGUS NICOL has lived in Shetland all his life and runs Sea Kayak Shetland. He has always enjoyed being on the water and frequently spent his weekends fishing from the family boat when he was young. Angus has a good knowledge and appreciation of the local environment and wildlife and respects the sea in all its moods. He is a coach at the local canoe club and also holds the new British Canoe Union four-star leader award.

If You Go

▶ **Getting There:** British Airways (800-247-9297; www.britishairways.com) books flights for the Shetlands via a number of Scottish cities.

▶ **Best Time to Visit:** June through August offer long days and calmer weather.

▶ **Guides/Outfitters:** Sea Kayak Shetland (+44 1595 84027; www.seakayakshetland.co .uk) offers day trips around the Shetlands.

▶ **Level of Difficulty:** Novice paddlers will be fine on guided trips; if you're planning to paddle the coastline on your own, you should have at least intermediate skills.

▶ **Accommodations:** Visit Shetland (visit.shetland.org) highlights lodging options.

DEVILS RIVER

RECOMMENDED BY **Marc McCord**

"The Devils River holds a magical spell over many people, especially paddlers," Marc McCord began. "Magazine stories have helped create an allure steeped in mystery and imagination that is unlike anything I know about any other river. I know a lot of people who have done a single trip there and never returned for a second shot at it. That is probably true of most people who venture there. Under optimum conditions, it is a very hard trip that most paddlers are simply not psychologically, mentally, or physically able to do. It flows through a harsh, sometimes hostile, environment where adjacent land-owners still think they own the river and where firearms are occasionally brandished or even fired over paddlers' heads. The headwinds off Lake Amistad can be a paddler's worst nightmare, and the place is a natural nesting area for rattlesnakes, scorpions, and other things that sting, bite, or stick you.

"This being said, I love the Devils River, and I have run it at least fifteen times. There are many things that make it special. There's the remoteness of the area, and the fact that fewer than six hundred people paddle it each year. The Devils is a long way from anywhere. Even if you live in Austin or San Antonio, it takes several hours to get there, so that discourages a lot of people from going. There's the incredible purity and clarity of the water and the natural beauty of this section of the Chihuahuan Desert. There's the quality of the fishing, which is among the best of any river in Texas. [Targets include smallmouth, largemouth, and Guadalupe bass.] And there's the overall challenge of running this undammed, free-flowing river—it really tests one's mettle for both planning and executing a wilderness river trip. Several of my friends have done multiple trips there with me, and we always welcome another opportunity to return."

OPPOSITE:
The Devils will
tax your skills
and endurance
as a paddler—
you'll either love
it or hate it!

DESTINATION

42

The Devils River flows approximately ninety miles through southwestern Texas. Fed by springs, it's considered the Lone Star State's most pristine river. First-timers and frequent visitors alike are always taken aback by the aquamarine hue of the river, a result of its limestone strata that leaches minerals into the water to give it an almost Caribbean blue. Portions of the upper section of the river run underground or run dry in the summer months, thus only the lower half—from Baker's Crossing to the Devils terminus at Lake Amistad, can be reliably run. Thanks to occasional skinny water and at least one portage (around Dolan Falls, a ten-plus-foot drop, depending on water levels), paddlers usually opt for canoes or kayaks to run the Devils. Given that the majority of the riverbanks are private property, visitors must camp at the three public camping areas along the river . . . and plan accordingly to reach them!

As Marc previously mentioned, the Devils' isolation, its limited access points, and its at-times inhospitable surroundings, all contribute to the challenges that the river serves up. The Devils' white water is not to be trifled with either. Marc described a few of its more inspiring (or daunting) runs. "Game Warden Rock (about thirteen miles below Baker's Crossing) is a true Class III rapid that has a hidden approach behind a reed jungle growing midriver. After clearing the reeds, you wind through a boulder channel about four to five feet wide before coming to a drop of about four feet with the namesake rock standing right in the middle of the channel. You have just seconds to decide on going left or right, and then executing the maneuver without pinning and wrapping your canoe or kayak on the rock. I should add that Game Warden Rock is not the only rapid hidden by reeds, though it's the only truly perilous one. The rest can better be described as inconveniences. The reed jungles are everywhere, and they can be eight to twelve feet tall. Some have multiple paths that are apparent from above, but not all of them are navigable because of shallow water and very narrow channels. Take the wrong channel and you will not get through. The reeds have blade-like edges that can easily slice open your skin. The trick is finding the proper channel that actually has navigable flows in wide-enough channels to get through without having to get out, walk your boat back upstream, and then try a different channel. The difficulty of navigating the reed jungles cannot be emphasized enough. Somebody who has never been there and cannot read a river will have extreme difficulty getting through the jungles, and even when you know what you are doing, it is slow, tiring work that will leave you exhausted and wondering why you ever went there in the first place.

DESTINATION

42

"Dolan Falls is your next obstacle, another three miles downstream. Luckily, it's easily visible well above the drop, so paddlers have an option of portaging on river left or right. The fall makes a gorgeous backdrop for photos after you unload boats, portage, and then reload. Three Tier Rapid, about one and a half miles below Dolan Falls, is a solid Class III+ run that is the most difficult on the river. The approach is through a reed jungle that opens into a channelized flat-water pool of calm water, where you can stop and scout the top of the drop. The entrance begins with a gradient slide of about twelve to fifteen feet over a distance of about twenty yards. Ideally, if the water is high enough, I run far left down a bone zone of boulders to the very bottom, where I make a hard ninety-degree left turn to start the run through the drops that make up the three tiers, each about two and a half feet, in quick succession. Going too far right at the top lines you up for a much more difficult run from the bottom of the slide and sets you up for a possible bow pin and capsize that sweeps your body down Three Tier, leaving behind skin on the very rough limestone river bottom."

The wind that can blow upriver off Lake Amistad is another wildcard in conquering the Devils.

"The wind, especially if coupled with low-water conditions, can dishearten even very stout and determined paddlers," Marc explained. "On one trip, four friends and I were trying to cover 8.3 miles. We had decent flows but encountered a headwind of about forty-five to fifty miles an hour the entire day. I have paddled marathon canoe races where I had to go 75 to 80 miles in twelve to fourteen hours, and my arms did not hurt as badly as they did from paddling that 8.3 miles in the headwinds of the Devils. We dared not stop paddling because the wind would blow us back upriver and make us cover the same distance again.

"They don't call it the Devils River for nothing—not even the devil himself would enjoy this river unless he was ready for a very hard workout."

Marc McCord first paddled a canoe in the Boy Scouts of America in the late 1950s. He got serious about paddling in 1975, when he did his first downriver trip on Oklahoma's scenic Illinois River near Tahlequah. Beginning in 1990, he became enthralled with paddling as a way of life, exploring wild and undeveloped rivers all over the southwestern United States. Marc has canoed over fifteen thousand miles in the past thirteen years. In 1997, he took the first of twelve swift-water rescue classes for added safety of himself and

189

42

his fellow paddlers on white-water rivers. Having led small private groups on canoe/camping trips for over a decade, he formed Canoeman River Guide Services in 2000 and began offering his experience to larger and more diverse groups that included companies, church and civic groups, scouting organizations, and private groups. Since 1996, Marc has been a web designer and has created several paddling-related websites for outfitters, retailers, and gear manufacturers, as well as his own projects that include Southwest Paddler, Lone Star Paddlers, and his personal site, Canoeman.com. Marc has experience building and training teams that work together for a common purpose, which led to the formation of team-building programs under the auspices of Canoeman River Guide Services.

If You Go

▶ **Getting There:** Baker's Crossing is approximately 200 miles from San Antonio and 280 miles from Austin, both of which are served by many major carriers.

▶ **Best Time to Visit:** Early spring to midsummer and early to midautumn are generally best. In the summer months, it will be very hot.

▶ **Guides/Outfitters:** Marc McCord (214-998-4922; www.canoeman.com) occasionally leads trips on the Devils if clients are truly committed.

▶ **Level of Difficulty:** This trip is recommended for expert paddlers with good outdoor skills and a strong sense of adventure.

▶ **Accommodations:** The Del Rio Chamber of Commerce (www.drchamber.com) lists lodging options in Del Rio, which is roughly an hour from the put-ins along the Devils.

PHANG NGA BAY AND BEYOND

RECOMMENDED BY **David Williams**

The beach paradises along the southwestern portion of Thailand's coast—including Phuket and Krabi—attract many international visitors, climbers, and paddlers among them. For some tastes, these spots may attract a few too many visitors. American expatriate David Williams suggests a somewhat different southern Thailand itinerary. "I love to show visiting kayakers Khao Sok National Park," he began. "It's a chance to experience a tropical jungle that's teeming with wildlife. After a few days exploring Khao Sok, we'll return to the coast and visit Phang Nga Bay Marine National Park. Most of the tour companies—more than a dozen of them—focus on three or four places in the bay. The result is similar to the road traffic in Bangkok. It's noisy, congested, and chaotic. Fortunately, they leave the northeast corner for me."

Khao Sok National Park is southern Thailand's largest reserve of virgin forest, situated a several hours' drive north of Phang Nga Bay. It's believed to have originated before the Amazonian rainforest and boasts one of the world's highest levels of biodiversity. The Chiao Lan reservoir sits in the midst of the almost three-hundred-square-mile preserve; this vast impoundment was formed with the creation of the Ratchaprapha Dam and will be the site of your paddling tour of the preserve. Upon reaching the dam, you'll board a long tail boat and motor approximately ninety minutes to a less visited section of the preserve. Your home for the next few days will be a floating bamboo bungalow. "A lot of outfitters talk about ecolodges, but these truly fit the bill," David described. "The bamboo couldn't be much more low impact—it's constantly degrading and in need of repair, but that's the idea of low impact. You can jump right off the deck and swim, and the lake is always the perfect temperature." (Meals are served in a small on-site restaurant and are more ambitious than the lodging.)

Over the next three or four days, you'll paddle along the shoreline of Chiao Lan in search of the many unique creatures that live in this untrammeled rainforest environment. "I like to get up with the sun, get a little coffee down the throat, and then get out on the water," David continued. The dawn calls of the gibbons often act as our alarm. Conventional wisdom is that the wildlife is most active around dawn and dusk. That being said, we often see animals that are supposed to be nocturnal right in the middle of the day." The list of species you may encounter in Khao Sok includes Malaysian tapir, Malaysian sun bear, guar (a species of wild bovine), pig-tailed macaque, gibbon, and mouse deer. "There's impressive birdlife, too, including great hornbills," David added. "They are massive birds, with wingspans of six or seven feet. Khao Sok has eight hornbill species present. The monkeys will often put on impressive acrobatics shows in the canopy. Dusky langurs do the best shows—they make incredible leaps with their babies clinging to them. One of the coolest wildlife displays I ever witnessed at Khao Sok was a mother and baby elephant that waded into the lake to play as my group came by. We paddled right up and watched until we got tired, at least forty-five minutes. Our presence didn't seem to bother them at all."

After returning to Phang Nga, it's time to head out in the bay. David likes to take paddlers out to the far northeastern section of the bay to an island called Koh Yao Noi. "Koh Yao Noi is inhabited mostly by Muslim fishermen," David said, "and it has maintained its cultural integrity despite being between Krabi and Phuket. We stay at family-owned bungalows on the island. They're a step up from the floating bungalows and have hot showers and air-conditioning." Some paddles depart from the island; others will use the motorized longboat to convey kayaks farther afield before dropping in. One appeal of paddling around Phang Nga is the chance to take in the otherworldly limestone karst formations that dot the bay. Many have hongs (Thai for rooms or caves) that you can paddle inside. There are also mangrove forests to explore and opportunities to meet subsistence fishermen on the water. The islands—including Koh Yao Noi—have interesting wildlife, including monitor lizards, barking deer, macaques, Oriental Pied hornbills, and a variety of kingfishers.

"I take a lot of school groups out on the bay," David reminisced. "These kids are rank beginners, have never kayaked, and may not have even been on the water before. They're pretty scared at first, but they overcome their fear. We'll often encounter fierce but brief squalls when we're out on the water. The wind will howl, and it will rain so hard that you

*OPPOSITE:
Many of
the limestone
karst islands in
Phang Nga Bay
have vast hongs
(caves).*

DESTINATION

43

can barely see a hundred yards out. When a storm blows through, I'll show them how to raft up and face right into the wind. The storms are always the kids' fondest memory of their time on the water. It's gratifying to see the kids learn not to panic and love every minute of it."

DAVID WILLIAMS is an American expatriate who has lived in Thailand since 1992. He is the only kayak tour operator in southern Thailand who was an expert-level paddler before getting in the paddling business. He started paddling in 1978 and has a great deal of experience in both serious white-water and sea kayaking. David has paddled all the most treacherous rivers in the eastern half of the United States and most of the dangerous rivers of Colorado. He also paddled 229 miles of the Grand Canyon in a squirt boat in 1989. He has, of course, paddled extensively in Thailand and in the rivers of Laos. David is a BCU (British Canoe Union) Level 2 coach and is Level 3 trained (Level 3 coach certificate to come shortly). He is also a BCU lifeguard, an Emergency First Response instructor, a Rescue 3 International rescue technician, and is ITC First Aid and CPR certified. David is a lifelong student of natural history, ornithology, biology, botany, paleontology, fitness, and Eastern philosophy. He majored in Eastern philosophy and music (as a percussionist) at Christopher Newport University in Newport News, Virginia.

If You Go

▶ **Getting There:** Trips generally stage in Phuket, which is served by a number of carriers, including Singapore Airlines (800-742-3333; www.singaporeair.com) and Thai Airways (800-426-5204; www.thaiair.com).

▶ **Best Time to Visit:** November through March offers cooler, less humid weather, though paddling opportunities are present throughout the year.

▶ **Guides/Outfitters:** A number of operators lead paddling tours on Phang Nga Bay, fewer on Khao Sok; Paddle Asia (+66.76.241.519; www.paddleasia.com) does both.

▶ **Level of Difficulty:** Paddling in both Khao Sok and Phang Nga Bay is well suited for beginners.

▶ **Accommodations:** Phuket.com lists many lodging options.

DESTINATION

43

HA'APAI & VAVA'U

RECOMMENDED BY **Sharon Spence**

Until Tonga joined the coalition of the willing in the Iraq War in 2003 (sending forty-odd troops to the conflict), many Americans might not have heard of this small island nation, let alone been able to place it on the map. Situated in the South Pacific about two-thirds of the way between Hawaii and New Zealand, Tonga consists of 169 coral atolls and volcanic islands, clustered in three main groups—Tongatapu to the south, Ha'apai in the center, and Vava'u to the north. Each has its own personality: Tongatapu is the nation's political center, home to much of the archipelago's population. The hilly and richly wooded islands of Vava'u enjoy the majority of Tonga's tourist trade. Ha'apai is less populated and developed than the other island groups and is felt to be the cultural center of the Tongan people. When Captain James Cook visited Tonga in the 1770s, he was so well received that he dubbed them "the Friendly Islands."

"When my husband and I began exploring potential places in the South Pacific to set up a paddling operation, Tonga had a singular appeal," Sharon Spence began. "It was the reefs. Vava'u is a smattering of fifty-odd islands with a semicircular reef that blocks the sea swells so most of the waterways are sheltered. Ha'apai is more of a true archipelago with islands stretching in a chain, though there are reefs between many of the islands. You can usually skirt the wind on the lee side. While they have reefs in common, the two island groups are radically different. Vava'u is hillier and hence more topographically interesting from a kayaker's perspective. In Vava'u, there's more tourism infrastructure. The Ha'apai Islands are flat and more windswept but have incredibly beautiful beaches. Because the local people here don't see as many tourists, they're generally friendlier, and they adhere to a more traditional lifestyle. (Tongan people in general are very friendly, though shy at first. Once you penetrate the shyness, they display a wicked sense of humor.) There aren't many amenities around Ha'apai, however, and the paddling here is better suited to a more adventurous kayaker."

A paddle about the Vava'u group of islands is ideally suited for less seasoned kayakers and offers some of the South Pacific's most stunning scenery. "I never tire of the views from the Port of Refuge," said Sharon. "It winds for a long way, like a Norwegian fjord, and is reputedly the most beautiful harbor in the South Pacific. I like to paddle into Swallows Cave—a misnomer since its residents are actually swiftlets—and snorkel amidst schools of zebra fish along a wall outside the cave entrance. One of my favorite campsites is at the eastern tip of Kapa Island. There are some wonderful coral gardens, and picture-perfect views across the channel of Nuku Island.

"Paddlers like to stretch their legs on a hike to the tabletop summit of uninhabited Euakafa Island, where there's a site of a royal tomb. (The legend goes that it was built by the king for his wife, whom he ordered to be beaten for courting a lover. Unfortunately, she was inadvertently beaten to death!) A highlight of a paddle about Vava'u is a visit to Taunga village, where the residents prepare a traditional Tongan feast exclusively for our group. As the meal is being prepared, the men sit around the kava bowl, pull out guitars, and sing romantic ballads about neighboring Euakafa Island and other legends of local interest. The meal includes a host of root crops (yam, taro, cassava), shellfish, pelagic fish, and octopus. Sometimes there's suckling pork, too. The octopus is very delicious when cooked in a pit, umu style, with coconut milk and onion."

Sharon spent most of her early paddling days around Vava'u, though in recent years, she's been spending more and more time at Ha'apai. An eleven-day island-hopping adventure has become one of her favorite trips, beginning at Pangai, and heading south down the Lifuka Archipelago. "There are many special points along the way," she described. "Early on, we stop and camp at a beach on the southern end of Uoleva Island that's been rated by *Outside* as one of the ten most beautiful beaches in the world. Weather permitting, I like to paddle to the remote island of Uanukuhahaki at the southern tip of the archipelago and camp there for a few days. This is a nesting ground for green turtles. I've been there on occasions when the turtles are coming up on the beach to bury their eggs, an event visitors find unforgettable. Snorkeling in the narrow channel between Uanukuhahaki and the adjacent small island is like swimming in a virtual aquarium of colorful fish and coral. The current sweeps you along, and the visibility is amazing—at least sixty feet. As we make our way back north, I enjoy stopping off at a tiny, uninhabited island called Luangahu. It's used by local fishermen, whose carved wood outrigger canoes are pulled up on the beach above the high-tide line. We'll often see their octopus-drying trees—limbs in the ground from which they hang their catch.

If you happen to visit Tonga between June and October, a special treat may await you—humpback whales. "The whales come from Antarctica to breed, give birth, and nurse their calves," Sharon explained. "I think they're the most interesting cetacean from a viewing perspective, as they're very active on the surface, with breaching, tail- and pectoral-fin slaps, and spy hopping [a behavior where the whale keeps its head out of the water to observe goings-on]. Historically, sightings of the humpbacks were most reliable around Vava'u, though in recent years, we see them more frequently around Ha'apai."

SHARON SPENCE and her husband, Doug, hail from the west coast of Canada but began exploring the South Pacific by sea kayak when they discovered the Vava'u Islands in 1988. Captivated by the natural beauty of this island paradise and the friendliness of its residents, they now operate adventure tours in the Kingdom of Tonga. World citizens, Sharon and Doug divide their team between Tonga and New Zealand's South Island.

If You Go

▶ **Getting There:** Visitors generally fly to Tongatapu first, which is served by Air Pacific (+676 24021; www.airpacific.com) and Air New Zealand (310-615-1111; www.airnewzealand.com). From Tongatapu, you'll need to fly to Vava'u/Ha'apai via REAL Tonga (+676 23777; www.realtonga.to).

▶ **Best Time to Visit:** Tonga's tropical climate sees a bit more humidity and rain between November and April, a bit more wind from May through October. Vava'u trips are led year-round; Ha'apai excursions, July through December.

▶ **Guides/Outfitters:** Friendly Islands Kayak Company (+64 3 4778635; www.fikco.com) leads trips around both the Vava'u and Ha'apai island groups.

▶ **Level of Difficulty:** Paddlers of modest ability will feel comfortable at Vava'u. Paddlers exploring Ha'apai should have at least a moderate skill level.

▶ **Accommodations:** If you go it on your own, the Tonga Visitors Bureau website (www.tongaholiday.com) highlights lodging options around Vava'u and Ha'apai.

DESTINATION

44

SOUTH GEORGIA ISLAND

RECOMMENDED BY **Rick Sweitzer**

Rick Sweitzer is celebrated in adventure travel circles for pushing the envelope in the realm of Arctic and Antarctic exploration. So it's no surprise that when asked about a favorite kayaking venue, he steered in a polar direction—specifically, South Georgia Island.

"We had been looking for exotic sub-Antarctic destinations to add to our polar offering," Rick began. "I had been thinking about Ernest Shackleton and his incredible adventure—the eight-hundred-mile crossing from Elephant Island, followed by a hike across South Georgia to the whaling station at Stromness. I thought it would be interesting to combine the passage across the South Atlantic and a tour of the shoreline of South Georgia with a re-creation of the overland portion of Shackleton's adventure."

South Georgia is one of the most isolated islands the world. It rests nearly 1,300 miles east of Tierra del Fuego and some 800 miles beyond the Falkland Islands, on the same latitudinal line as Cape Horn. South Georgia Island itself is long and narrow, roughly 100 miles long and alternating from just 1 mile to 25 miles in width. Several mountain ranges extend along its center; there are eleven peaks greater than 6,500 feet. During the island's brief summer, most of the ground remains cloaked in glaciers, ice caps, and snowfields; icebergs dot the coastline. The first European to eye South Georgia was a London merchant named Anthony de la Roché, who took shelter near the island in 1675 after losing his way around Cape Horn. One hundred years later, Captain Cook came upon the island, thinking he had finally identified the last great continent. He was, of course, mistaken, and he named the island for King George. Cook's reports of great numbers of whales and seals in the waters around South Georgia brought first sealers and then whalers. The whaling onslaught began in earnest in the early 1900s. The world's greatest concentration

OPPOSITE:
Seals, sea lions,
elephant seals,
and countless
birds await
kayakers in
what's been called
"the Galápagos of
the South Seas."

DESTINATION

45

of whales—blue, fin, sei, humpback, and southern right—were reduced to a mere 10 percent (or less) of their former populations. (In 1974, these species received protection under the International Whaling Commission, and their numbers are slowly increasing.) Sperm whales and orcas, less impacted by industrialized whaling, are also seen in the waters off South Georgia. At the heyday of the whaling boom, two thousand people called South Georgia home; now it has no permanent inhabitants.

What South Georgia lacks in human population it more than makes up for in bird and pinniped biomass. Eighty-one different bird species have been documented on the island, including albatrosses, cape and giant petrels, Antarctic prions, and many, many, many macaroni, gentoo, and king penguins. Scientists place the island's seabird population at more than thirty million! Though hunted to near extinction during the nineteenth century, both elephant seals and fur seals have recovered marvelously; the fur seal population is placed at over three million. "The masses of wildlife along the shoreline can be simply overwhelming," professional sailor, mountaineer, and explorer Skip Novak has said. "Sometimes you'll go close to shore and there will be hundreds of thousands of these animals." Deep in the South Atlantic, you are always at the whim of the weather. You move and go ashore when conditions permit. "There have been times at South Georgia when I'm trying to lead my sailboat from one anchorage to another," Novak added. "It's blowing like hell, and with the fog and/or snow, you can't see anything. You're cold, exhausted, utterly spent. Eventually, you get to the next anchorage and more or less collapse. As I fall asleep on such nights, I'm wondering, 'What are we doing here!?!' The next morning, I wake up to beautiful, bright conditions, and the boat is surrounded by seals and penguins. I sit with a cup of coffee or tea and reflect on this place of great contrasts."

The beauty of South Georgia was not likely lost on Ernest Shackleton, though during his 1916 visit, he had more pressing matters to deal with . . . like survival. On an expedition to Antarctica, his ship, the *Endurance*, had been trapped and eventually crushed by ice. After surviving nearly a year on ice floes with his twenty-seven men, Shackleton led his crew to Elephant Island in three lifeboats. The trip took five days. Realizing there was little hope of rescue on desolate Elephant Island, Shackleton and five crewmen boarded the most durable of the lifeboats—the *James Caird*—and set sail for South Georgia, eight hundred nautical miles' distance across the Scotia Sea. Miraculously, two weeks later they landed at uninhabited King Haakon Bay. After a brief rest, Shackleton and two of his comrades set out to cross the island toward Stromness Bay, where there was a whaling station. Their route had never been taken, and dangerous glaciers, crisscrossed with crevasse fields, stood between them and their destination, but the men made the thirty-two miles in just thirty-six hours. Soon after, they retrieved the three men they'd left at King Haakon Bay and returned to Elephant Island to rescue the remaining crew members. Thanks to Shackleton's bravery and good judgment, no lives were lost.

"We wanted to follow Shackleton's path as closely as possible, from King Haakon Bay to Stromness," Rick continued, "though we did try to avoid the wrong turns. And we did the thirty-two miles over four days. We had skis and other modern equipment, and plenty of food. Shackleton had no compass, no gear—just some rope. When you come down to Stromness Bay, you have this amazing sense of how it must have felt for his party to come upon the whaling station after all they'd been through. It's a chance to share the spirit of the pioneering days of the Antarctic."

Once the overland portion of his adventure was completed, Rick was eager to do some paddling. "They call South Georgia the Galápagos of the Southern Seas, and I wanted to get out among the amazing bird and marine mammal life," he said. "I slid past throngs of sea lions, fur seals, and penguins, past bays where glaciers were calving. At one point, I paddled past the world's largest colony of elephant seals—some of them sixteen feet long [and weighing up to four tons]. It was breeding time, and the bulls were squaring off to defend their harems.

"As I was paddling among the seals and sea lions near Stromness Bay, there were some passengers from a cruise ship up onshore. I found myself thinking of Captain Cook sailing around this island almost 250 years ago. I wasn't the first to ply the waters around South Georgia Island, but not many have done so."

RICK SWEITZER has been leading winter mountaineering and ski expeditions for the last thirty years. In 1993, he created, organized, and coguided the first-ever dogsled and ski expedition to the North Pole for amateur adventurers. Since then, he has guided dozens of expeditions to the North and South Poles and another half dozen flights to the North Pole. He is executive director of PolarExplorers and founder of the Northwest Passage, an adventure travel company that guides trips around the world.

DESTINATION

45

► **Getting There:** Many adventures to South Georgia begin in Ushuaia, Argentina, which is served by Aerolíneas Argentinas (800-333-0276; www.aerolineas.com.ar) via Buenos Aires. Northwest Passage's tour departs from Montevideo, Uruguay, which is also served by Aerolíneas Argentinas.

► **Best Time to Visit:** The austral spring and summer, November through mid-March.

► **Guides/Outfitters:** Several outfitters offer trips to South Georgia. Northwest Passage (800-256-4409; www.nwpassage.com) is offering the trip that follows in the footsteps of Ernest Shackleton and will include some paddling.

► **Level of Difficulty:** This is primarily a wildlife/adventure cruise with some paddling. Significant paddling experience is not required.

► **Accommodations:** The Fuegian Institute of Tourism (www.tierradelfuego.org.ar) lists lodging options in Ushuaia.

HA LONG BAY

RECOMMENDED BY **Patrick Morris**

The imposing and spectacular limestone pillars of Ha Long Bay create a seascape that's unlike anything anywhere in the world. Larger ships cruise the bay, affording panoramic views of these surreal karst landforms, some cloaked in vegetation, others rising like gray obelisks into the sky. And when you hop into a kayak, you're able to paddle right up to these strange islands, and in some cases, through the middle of them.

"The geography of Ha Long is certainly an important reason to come," began Patrick Morris. "Until you see the islands, you can't believe how over the top they are. But everyone who visits leaves impressed with the spirit and good nature of the Vietnamese people and the insights into the culture that you can experience out on the water. The Vietnamese are a very informal people and have a largely classless society, and I think that aspect of their culture is very familiar to Americans. Their energy levels are tremendous and their good humor is infectious. At the moment, Vietnam is in a state of flux, and the juxtapositions between ancient and new are amazing. In Hanoi, you'll see older farmers from the country wearing conical hats and slippers selling vegetables on the street as young people clutching iPads pass them en route to cafés to do work for new start-ups. The last vestiges of the older culture are still there, but they are fading quickly, and if you wish to see them, there's an urgency to visit soon.

"From a kayaking perspective, there are two things that surprise people about Ha Long Bay. First, they are amazed at the bay's placid conditions. The hundreds of islands serve to break up the swells from the South China Sea. Occasionally there's a surge of current, but for the most part it's like a swimming pool, delightfully calm. And the water is always temperate, even in the cooler season. The other surprise is how affordable it is to do a kayaking excursion on Ha Long, especially if you go on a smaller boat.

As kayaking trips go, it's in the 'backpacker' category in terms of expense."

Ha Long Bay sits on the western edge of the Gulf of Tonkin in Quang Ninh Province, not far from Vietnam's border with China; it's roughly a hundred miles southeast of Hanoi. The coastline of Ha Long—which translates as "Descending Dragon Bay"—stretches roughly seventy miles, and its six hundred square miles are dotted with more than two thousand islands, islets, and pillars—some jagged, some rounded, most unpopulated, and all on the edge of the bizarre. These otherworldly karst formations—which entered the broader consciousness in the James Bond film *The Man with the Golden Gun*—are the result of millions of years of sculpting by the South China Sea. After twenty years of exploring Ha Long, Patrick has some thoughts for paddlers interested in exploring this UNESCO World Heritage Site. "Some people who are touring Vietnam try to sandwich in a little kayaking on the bay while they're making their way north or south from Hanoi. I think this is a mistake for two reasons: First, you miss the sunsets and sunrises, which, I feel, are the most incredible times to be on the water. Second, you don't have time to get very far away from Ha Long City. You hear some people complain about the crowds on Ha Long Bay, and if you don't get far out beyond the port area, that's certainly true, as it is almost anywhere in the world. But if you get just a little farther out—which you have time to do on a multiday trip—you can escape the packs of cruise ships and find solitude among the many islands."

Multiday trips on Ha Long Bay are conducted from motherships, where you'll sleep and take your meals. These are not sleek fiberglass yachts but wooden cruisers of moderate size. "The government of Vietnam doesn't allow foreign operators, so all the boats are made here," Patrick continued. "There's quite a bit of variation in the quality of the crafts and their level of maintenance. But if you choose carefully, the experience of getting to know the crew is worth the adventure in itself. The young men who work on the boats have a tremendous sense of humor and are often playing jokes. They make elaborate fruit and vegetable carvings with papaya, pineapples, whatever they have handy. They're artists, and they're happy to show you how to carve. The Vietnamese love to gamble, and at night, you can watch them play cards, or even join a hand.

"Once you get out away from the crowds, it's time to drop the kayaks in and explore the islands up close. Many of the karst formations have caves. I still recall the first time I made my way into one of these caves, only to find a hidden lake in the middle. There I was, out in the middle of the bay, in a lake within a limestone tower that I reached

OPPOSITE:
Paddlers in
Ha Long Bay
encounter
otherworldly
karst formations
and floating
fisherman
"villages."

46

DESTINATION

through a cave. It was one of the most interesting experiences I've ever had. Another feature I love about Ha Long is that most of the karst islands have little coves with white-sand beaches. They're incredibly picturesque, and you can ease in with a kayak and relax in your own deserted cove, have a picnic, or take a swim. I always make it a point to visit one of the floating fisherman's villages that you find on the bay. These aren't temporary camps; they're where people live. They even have dogs. The fishermen and their families are very welcoming. If you tie up, you'll be invited inside and served green tea. Our guides will translate; we'll learn what they're fishing for—squid, cuttlefish, crabs, or other fish. If the fishermen are around [some fish at night], they might be doing karaoke—an omni-present facet of Vietnam! Sometimes, the fishermen will have nets strewn between the decks of their boats to keep their catch alive until it can be sold. It's like a little fish farm."

For many visitors to Vietnam, meals are a central part of the experience. It's no differ-ent on Ha Long Bay. "The crew members on the boats I've chartered are incredible cooks," Patrick said. "Breakfast is fresh fruit, wonderful omelets, pho, and 'depth charge' Vietnamese coffee. Spring rolls, French fries, and baguettes are staples [the latter, of course, a remnant of French rule]; the guys are happy to show you how to make spring rolls. As we're cruising to a new spot in the bay, fishermen will come up to sell us their catch. It's interesting to watch the captain haggle with them. Some of the specimens look unfamiliar; the prawns are as a big as your hand! Dinner entrees include tuna with a tomato and onion sauce or cubed steak with onions and green papaya salad. [Vegetarian dishes are also available.] The chicken and beef are tasty but very lean, as the animals aren't fattened up. We call the fowl Olympic chickens—they're skinny and always run-ning like mad."

PATRICK MORRIS organized and led the first cycling tours of Vietnam some twenty years ago. After over *twenty thousand* miles of cycling in Vietnam and working on country projects with the U.S. Agency for International Aid and the U.S. Trade and Development Agency, there are few guides who know Vietnam better. Patrick pioneered many of Vietnam's original adventure trips, including biking in Sapa and the central highlands. Patrick has contributed to almost every guidebook written on Vietnam but believes that the real highlight of the country is the limitless optimism, warmth, and incessant humor of the Vietnamese people.

▶ **Getting There:** The trip begins in Hanoi, which is served by many carriers, including Cathay Pacific (800-233-2742; www.cathaypacific.com).

▶ **Best Time to Visit:** You can paddle Ha Long Bay throughout the year, though December through June generally offers the best combination of moderate temperatures and less precipitation. (Try to avoid monsoon season in September and October.)

▶ **Guides/Outfitters:** A number of companies lead kayaking adventures on Ha Long Bay, including VeloAsia (888-681-0808; www.veloasia.com).

▶ **Level of Difficulty:** Ha Long Bay is great for beginners, as there are hardly any waves or currents.

▶ **Accommodations:** In Hanoi, the Sofitel Legend Metropole Hanoi (+84 438266919; www.sofitel.com) comes well recommended.

LITTLE WHITE SALMON RIVER

RECOMMENDED BY **Nicole Mansfield**

Nicole Mansfield had been packing and unpacking her bags every three months or so for the past ten years. A few runs down the Little White Salmon convinced her to set down some roots . . . at least for now.

"I spent three summers traveling on the white-water kayaking circuit and had been living seasonally all over for years before that, trying to find the perfect spot to live, with awesome skiing and kayaking," Nicole began. "Friends on the circuit were always talking about the Little White Salmon, and when we came up to Washington, they took me down the river. I was pretty scared the first time but came away thinking it was a magical place—crystal water, beautiful gorges, and awesome rapids. Thanks to the river and the great paddling community in the White Salmon area, I chose to move here. It's the first place I've ever lived for a year since leaving college. That's a big deal for me!"

The Little White Salmon is a short river—19 miles—that flows swiftly in a narrow canyon out of the Gifford Pinchot National Forest, dumping into the Columbia River roughly 60 miles east of Portland, Oregon . . . or 160 miles from the Pacific. (It's roughly across the Columbia from Hood River, which has gained no small amount of notoriety for windsurfing and kiteboarding.) A lot of rain falls in this section of the Columbia River Gorge in the winter months, and that works to the Little White's advantage; it's fed by an aquifer that is in turn fed by the rains. This results in very consistent flows of superbly translucent blue water, allowing intrepid paddlers to run it well into the summer.

Intrepid . . . and very skilled. The Little White Salmon is for Class V paddlers only. And even professional-level kayakers have lost their lives here; it's considered the most difficult regularly run river in the west.

OPPOSITE:
Kayaker Evan Garcia takes the thirty-plus-foot plunge at Spirit Falls—not for your casual paddler!

DESTINATION

47

Considering its proximity to civilization and many skilled paddlers, it may be surprising to some that the Little White did not see its first descent until the early 1990s. After a quick review of its obstacles—a mix of unrelenting boulder gardens and dizzying drops, including thirty-three-foot Spirit Falls, all squeezed into 4.3 miles of canyon—you begin to understand why. Advances in kayaking technology, from polyethylene boats to improved dry suits, have emboldened more and more paddlers to take the plunge. Yet no equipment breakthrough or heightened level of audaciousness is a substitute for expertise . . . an expertise Nicole and her cohorts possess. She went on to describe an average Little White morning.

"When the river is running well—especially in winter and spring—I'll often wake up and text my roommate (Katrina Van Wijk), 'Little White?' We may have some couch surfers in the house, and if they're game, we'll put some coffee on and head out early. If we don't have guests, a few more texts to local paddlers are enough to assemble a crew to head out. At a place like the Gauley [River in West Virginia], everyone camps at the put-in. Here, there's an established community, places where visiting paddlers can crash (like the Beaver Lodge) and nice hidden camping spots. We'll meet at the take-out, which is at Drano Lake. Sometimes I'll get there expecting to find five people and there will be fifteen. It's only about a ten-minute drive from the take-out to the put-in at the National Fish Hatchery. You could walk if you had to. (There's a section above the put-in that you can run at high water, but most people run from the bridge to Drano.) The first half mile is a fairly easy—Class II/III—boulder garden. There's no rest from here on. First you come to the Getting Busy Rapid. To me, this is one of the most technical sections of the run, a half-mile, continuous boulder garden. It's game-on instantly, and there's no messing around. It's a maze. I followed people through the first twenty times; now I can make it down on my own.

"After Getting Busy, you come into what I think of as quintessential Little White Salmon—a stretch of beautiful waterfalls. There are a number of them, and you can take all sorts of different lines. This keeps things fresh." The ledges begin modestly (for the Little White), starting with Sacrilege (a ten-footer) and Double Drop (a pair of five-footers). S-Turn is the first of the river's signature falls, plunging fourteen feet into a soft pool. Wishbone is not much farther along; here, boaters are launched eighteen feet into The Gorge, which ends in Horseshoe, a six-foot drop with some gnarly hydraulics. "All of the falls have fun boulder gardens in between," Nicole added. "It's not just pool-drop, pool-drop; it's continuous white water all the time."

The Little White's waterfalls build to stunning culmination at Spirit Falls, which plummets thirty to thirty-five feet, depending on water levels. "It's definitely the river's signature waterfall, a perfect flume that drops into a big pool surrounded by mossy cliffs," Nicole described. "A lot of people hike in just to see the falls. Most paddlers used to portage it, but I'd say more than half the people run it now. I love the feeling of the free fall. The challenge is finding a good angle to land on. I'm always trying to find forty-five degrees; if you land flat, you have a chance of breaking your back. It's a great feeling to look back and see where you've come from, though you don't have long to think about it, as the lead out, Chaos, requires some thought. There's one more rough rapid, Master Blaster, another boulder garden, that may be my least favorite part of the run. It can get you in weird ways. Then you go over a few fish ladders and down into Drano Lake. A five-minute paddle across the lake—where you'll sometimes see huge salmon swimming around you—and you're done.

"Some people do the Little White in forty-five minutes and will run two or three laps regularly in a day. If you're taking your time and savoring the experience, it can be made into a full day trip . . . especially with some scouting and picture taking. Some people come down planning to run it once, and when they reach the take-out, they run into a bunch of friends just arriving . . . so they decide to go again. If there was a food cart at the take-out, it would make a killing." Next best is one of the Little White's popular hangouts, Everybody's Brewing. Post paddling, Nicole likes a Country Boy IPA and a plate of nachos.

"There's a special moment for me when I truly appreciate where I am and what I'm doing," Nicole offered. "It comes at this little calm spot between Wishbone and The Gorge. It's a place where people might stop for a moment and empty out their boats or wait for friends to come by. You're feeling a little bit of anxiety about what's to come, a surge of adrenaline from what's just happened . . . and you're surrounded by all the reasons I enjoy paddling the river. Crystal clear waters, green moss, good friends, and the imposing gorge walls."

NICOLE MANSFIELD graduated from Dartmouth College in 2005 and has spent all of her post-college life skiing and kayaking. Her kayaking adventures have taken her around the world, including South America, Africa, Europe, and New Zealand. She competed in her first Little White Salmon Race in 2013 and numerous rodeos and races

DESTINATION

47

around the United States and abroad, and is sponsored by NRS, Pyranha, Astral Buoyancy, Werner Paddles, and Five Ten. As of this writing, she calls White Salmon, Washington, home.

If You Go

▶ **Getting There:** The Little White Salmon flows into the Columbia near the town of White Salmon, which is roughly an hour east of Portland, Oregon.

▶ **Best Time to Visit:** The Little White generally has enough water from November through late July.

▶ **Guides/Outfitters:** You'll have to go it alone on the Little White Salmon. But if you've got the chops and show up in the village of White Salmon, it won't be hard to find some local paddlers to show you the way (try Everybody's Brewing for starters).

▶ **Level of Difficulty:** Extreme! Only attempt this if you're a seasoned Class V kayaker.

▶ **Accommodations:** The Inn of the White Salmon (800-972-5226; www.innofthewhite salmon.com) offers both standard rooms and hostel-style lodging.

SAN JUAN ISLANDS

RECOMMENDED BY **Tom Murphy**

"I like to think that the San Juans offer paddlers the best of both worlds," Tom Murphy opined. "You can get out into the natural environment under your own power while only being a couple of hours from the Space Needle. The cold, constantly circulating water here makes for an incredible density of life; it's off the charts. The nutrient-rich waters foster phytoplankton, which in turn foster animal life all the way up the food chain to orcas. Sea kayaks make it possible to carry more than when you are backpacking. You can bring along a few extras to make your camping experience that much more comfortable."

The San Juan archipelago begins north of Puget Sound, roughly sixty miles north of Seattle, and stretches nearly a hundred miles. Resting between Vancouver Island and the Strait of Juan de Fuca to the west, the Strait of Georgia to the north, and the mainland of Washington to the east, the islands were the historical home of the Salish people, who traveled from island to island in cedar canoes, subsisting primarily on salmon; indeed, the inland waters are known as the Salish Sea. There are upward of seven hundred islands in the San Juan chain, though most of the area's residents live on the four largest islands—Orcas, San Juan, Lopez, and Shaw. (Some of the islands in the archipelago rest in Canadian territory and are called the Gulf Islands.) The San Juans are remnants of ancient mountain ranges that geologists believe were once part of a separate continent, one that predates North America. Resting in the rain shadow of the Olympics, the climate of the islands is in stark contrast to the rest of western Washington; the San Juans see more sunshine and only half the rain of Seattle. The terrain—rocky bays and inlets framed by thick conifer forests—is reminiscent of the coastline of downeast Maine . . . with the addition of snowcapped mountains (including Mount Baker and Mount Rainier) looming in the distance. It's a lush, temperate landscape with enough human settlement

DESTINATION

48

to make provisioning easy but enough isolation to give one exposure to a unique marine environment and ecosystem.

"The tone for a visit to the San Juans is set when you step on the ferry," Tom continued. "I think it gives you a sense of breaking away from your routine. Most people's lives are rush-rush-rush, but once you get on the ferry, you have no choice but to let things slow down." On a three-day paddle around the San Juans, life will slow down considerably more. Tom described one of his favorite itineraries, a roughly thirty-mile expedition from San Juan Island to Stuart Island. "We'll drive out to the west side of San Juan and drop our boats in at San Juan Park. We'll begin paddling north. Depending on the tide/ current, we'll take either an inside or outside route. On the inside route, we're able to be very close to shore; there are no breaking waves because Vancouver Island protects us from the open Pacific. I love seeing the small-scale microcosms on the rocks—barnacles, mussels, oysters—up close. We'll also keep an eye offshore, too, as this is prime orca habitat. [The region is home to three resident groups—the J, K, and L pods—that make up eighty-five to ninety animals. Researchers and whale enthusiasts can identify each animal by the shape of its dorsal fin and its "saddle patch," the mammal's trademark gray markings.] To the south, we have wonderful views of the Olympic Mountains on the Olympic Peninsula; to the west, we can see Vancouver Island."

After lunch, paddlers cross the Spieden Channel. "It's one of the longer crossings that we do on our trips, roughly an hour to one and half hours out on the open water," Tom continued. "You're a mile or more from shore, but it's calm. There are big tides, and because of the bottlenecks that the islands form, there are some tricky currents in places. Our guides take the guesswork out of timing the tides and currents."

Home for the next two nights will be a campsite on Stuart Island at a sheltered spot called Reid Harbor. It's part of the Cascadia Marine Trail, a series of fifty-five state park camping facilities for human-wind-powered beachable watercraft, which extends from the southern reaches of Puget Sound to the San Juans. "Stuart Island has some great hikes," Tom said. "If you head to the northwest part of the island, you'll eventually reach the Turn Point Light Station. It's the most northwesterly point in the continental United States. There's another vista point nearby called Lover's Leap that has nesting peregrine falcons. After a comfortable night in camp, we circumnavigate Stuart Island. It gives everyone a chance to see some amazing shoreline that you can't access from land. We try to make our trips a walk in the park rather than a race up the mountain, with the emphasis being on enjoying the beautiful surroundings rather than grinding out miles. In the evening, you have the option of doing a 'bioluminescence paddle.' Seeing the single-celled microfauna make the water glow highlights just how much life is here." On a four-day trip, paddlers might also visit uninhabited Jones Island. "If we go to Jones, it's fun to do a hike that circumnavigates the island, and then circumnavigate the island again by kayak," Tom added. "You get very different perspectives from land and water."

"It's a special feeling to be out on Jones or Stuart Island in the evening. You got there under your own power, have good food in your belly, and you're watching a beautiful sunset."

TOM MURPHY has guided paddlers in the San Juan Islands since 2001. He graduated from Lawrence University in 2003 with a biology degree. After graduation, Tom spent a year and a half overseas, traveling through India, working for a nongovernmental organization in Nepal, and teaching science to elementary students in the outdoor classroom of the Swiss Alps. In the winter months, Tom is an avid backcountry skier and brand ambassador for Seattle-based Outdoor Research. In the summer, he operates his company Outdoor Odysseys, one of the oldest and most respected kayak outfitter in the San Juans.

If You Go

▶ **Getting There:** Ferry service is available from Anacortes (ninety miles north of Seattle), operated by the Washington Department of Transportation (www.wsdot.wa.gov/ferries). Plane service is available on San Juan Airlines (www.sanjuanairlines.com).

▶ **Best Time to Visit:** The most pleasant kayaking conditions will be encountered from mid-May through mid-October.

▶ **Guides/Outfitters:** A number of kayaking companies offer tours of the San Juans, including Outdoor Odysseys (800-647-4621; www.outdoorodysseys.com).

▶ **Level of Difficulty:** Less seasoned paddlers will generally feel comfortable in the San Juans.

▶ **Accommodations:** The San Juan Islands Visitors Bureau (888-468-3701; www.visit sanjuans.com) provides a comprehensive list of lodging options on the San Juans should you decide to stay a few extra days.

DESTINATION

48

NEW AND GAULEY RIVERS

RECOMMENDED BY **Rick Johnson**

The state of West Virginia has trademarked the following phrase:

America's Best Whitewater

There are some tourism departments in the American west that might take some exception to this claim. Though with the New and Gauley Rivers cascading within an hour of each other toward their confluence—and several other Class IV/V rivers nearby—the Mountain State has a strong case.

"The New and the Gauley are on many people's lists of top-ten single-day white-water rafting rivers," Rick Johnson began. "Both have reliable flows, thanks to dam releases, and both have pleasantly warm water. We raft rainwater, not snowmelt. Both rivers are of a pool/drop nature, so you have a moment to catch your breath between rapids. In the case of the New, you have bigger water than you'll find on the west coast. If you come down to visit, you can run both rivers in a weekend. And since we're within eight hours' drive of most major cities in the northeast and southeast, more than a few people do."

The sections of the New and Gauley Rivers of greatest interest to paddlers both reside in the southern section of West Virginia. They join in the town of Gauley Bridge to form the Kanawha, which in turn flows into the Ohio River. The New is the longer, and overall more powerful, of the two rivers. It begins in the Appalachians of western North Carolina and flows in a northerly direction roughly 320 miles, passing through southern Virginia before reaching West Virginia. The name is somewhat misleading; geologists believe that the New is actually one of the three oldest rivers in the world; the moniker came from seventeenth-century explorers, as the river was "new" to them. The West Virginia portion of the New offers a variety of experiences. The upper section is calmer and best for mellow floats and fishing; the middle adds some more adventurous rapids to the mix; the

OPPOSITE:

It takes serious skills to navigate the Upper Gauley (Pillow Rock rapids shown here) during "Gauley Season."

DESTINATION

49

lower runs through the New Gorge and is the section of greatest interest to white-water enthusiasts. "The New and its surrounding canyon helped build America," Rick continued. "As you make your way down, you pass by many old coal camps where thousands of people once lived, back in the time when coal was king."

The Gauley has earned the intriguing (and intimidating) sobriquet "the Beast of the East," and draws rafters from across North America and beyond. It begins in the Monongahela National Forest, near the Virginia border, and flows 105 miles before joining the New. The 10-mile stretch of river directly below the impoundment at Summersville Lake—known as the Upper Gauley—is the main attraction, though people will run other parts of the river as well. Excitement really builds with the arrival of Labor Day weekend: For the next six weekends, the Army Corp of Engineers ramps up water releases expressly to make the upper Gauley a white-water wonderland. Those in the know refer to this shoulder period bridging summer and autumn as "Gauley Season." "Like the New, the Gauley is steeped in history," Rick added. "It was the site of a Civil War battle [Carnifex Ferry in 1861, where Union troops drove Confederate soldiers back across the Gauley] and a major logging area. The upper gets most of the attention for the big water, but the Lower Gauley is just beautiful beyond compare. You're floating past these huge boulders the size of cars, with the canyon walls climbing three hundred feet. The upper river is pretty, too, but it's so fast-paced, you don't really have much time to enjoy the scenery."

The Lower New (from Cunard to Fayette Station) runs roughly seven miles and includes eighteen rapids of Class III or more in that compact space. A few of the New's best tests include the Kenneys (upper, middle, and lower); Double Z (the most technical rapid on the river—you'll know you're getting close when you see a rock that resembles a thumb); and Fayette Station (a last hurrah of large waves before the take-out). "The New is great for doing a little surfing, West Virginia–style," Rick said. "My favorite rapids for surfing are Greyhound Bus Stopper, Lower Railroad, and Bloody Nose in Miller's Folly."

The Upper Gauley packs twenty-nine rapids of Class III or greater into ten exhilarating miles. These include the "Big Five," five Class V rapids named Insignificant (which is how an early paddler described it, relative to what was to come); Pillow (anything but soft and restful); Lost Paddle (a grueling mile-long run that consists of four drops); Iron Ring (loggers had placed a large iron ring in a nearby rock; it's gone now); and Sweet's Falls (named for John Sweet, a competitive paddler who first ran the fourteen-foot falls in 1968 . . . with a canoe!). "When I drop Sweet's Falls and look back up, there's usually a rainbow from the light filtering through the spray that's kicking up," Rick described. "Your adrenaline is really pumping from the drop, but then there's the peace and beauty of the rainbow."

West Virginia has never been an easy place to eke out a living. But activities like paddling keep hope alive for a better future. "West Virginia's story is the story of survival," Rick offered. "The extractive industries here—lumber, coal—they come and go. The money these industries generated didn't stay in Appalachia. Tourism is a resource that renews itself. And the money stays here and gives families a chance to make a go of it."

RICK JOHNSON and his wife, Heather, own River Expeditions—one of West Virginia's largest white-water rafting outfitters on the New and Gauley Rivers. Since 1996, Rick has maintained a hands-on approach to running his business and is involved in day-to-day operations. He chairs subcommittees on the West Virginia Whitewater Commission and the West Virginia Division of Tourism, and is on the board of directors for the West Virginia Professional River Outfitters Association.

If You Go

▶ **Getting There:** Most visitors will fly into Charleston, West Virginia, which is served by a number of carriers. From here, it's roughly ninety miles to the river hubs.

▶ **Best Time to Visit:** The New flows highest in the spring but can be run through October; the Gauley is at its prime from early September through mid-October.

▶ **Guides/Outfitters:** A number of companies offer paddles on the New and Gauley Rivers, including River Expeditions (800-463-9873; www.raftinginfo.com).

▶ **Level of Difficulty:** Beginners are fine on guided trips; only the most seasoned paddlers will want to attempt the New or Gauley on their own.

▶ **Accommodations:** River Expeditions offers a variety of lodging options; West Virginia Division of Tourism (800-225-5982; www.wvtourism.com) highlights other options.

DESTINATION

49

ZAMBEZI RIVER

RECOMMENDED BY **John Berry**

In November of 1855, Dr. David Livingstone first set his eyes upon the flumes of spray rising from what would become known as Victoria Falls:

> After twenty minutes' sail from Kalai we came in sight, for the first time, of the columns of vapor appropriately called "smoke," rising at a distance of five or six miles, exactly as when large tracts of grass are burned in Africa. Five columns now arose, and, bending in the direction of the wind, they seemed placed against a low ridge covered with trees; the tops of the columns at this distance appeared to mingle with the clouds. They were white below, and higher up became dark, so as to simulate smoke very closely. The whole scene was extremely beautiful; the banks and islands dotted over the river are adorned with sylvan vegetation of great variety of color and form . . . no one can imagine the beauty of the view from anything witnessed in England. It had never been seen before by European eyes; but scenes so lovely must have been gazed upon by angels in their flight.

Known as *Mosi-oa-Tunya* ("the smoke that thunders" in the Lozi language) among the local Bantu people, the falls are just as awe-inspiring a sight today. But for adrenaline junkies, it's the falls' downriver handiwork that attracts even greater attention. Twenty-three rapids—including a number of Class Vs—await you in one action-packed day.

"The Zambezi is widely considered the wildest and most spectacular single-day white-water rafting trip in the world," John Berry began. "It can be run almost year-round, though the wildest runs come in November and December, during the lowest water. Beyond the rapids, there's the power of Victoria Falls. In the gorge, you can feel it reverberating in your chest."

OPPOSITE:
The stretch of the Zambezi below Victoria Falls boasts twenty-three hair-raising rapids, making it one of the greatest one-day white-water trips in the world.

221

At 1,600 miles in length, the Zambezi River is Africa's fourth-longest river. It rises in northwestern Zambia and flows through the countries of Angola, Botswana, Zimbabwe, and finally to Mozambique, where it empties into the Indian Ocean. It's hard to overstate the grandeur of Victoria Falls, which stretch more than a mile across and boast a maximum drop of over 350 feet into the Batoka Gorge, making it the world's largest sheet of falling water . . . and one of the Seven Natural Wonders of the World. "The rafting day begins with a twenty-minute hike down to the river," John continued. "Many of the people who go on day trips may not have had much rafting experience, so we do a little paddling lesson on a large pool below the falls and brief everyone on how to recover if they end up going for a swim. Some guests are frightened once they actually get down to the river and strap on their life vest. We make it clear that you're not in mortal danger, but you are certainly going to have an adrenaline overload." (If you get a particularly early start, you might want to observe the falls from the top. At a spot called the Devil's Armchair, you can safely swim to the edge of the falls and peer right over the edge, where the river drops 300 feet.)

The first few rapids on the Zambezi allow for a bit of a warm-up but begin to intensify at Rapid 4, Morning Glory, a crashing center wave with gaping holes right and left. (All the rapids are known by numbers and nicknames.) The first Class V, Stairway to Heaven, follows. It's a maze of crashing waves that's been likened to dropping off a two-story building. Rapid 7, Gullivers Travels, is the next Class V and is the longest rapid in the gorge, requiring several moves before you reach the Land of Giants, a series of haystack waves that usher you forth. Most paddlers (and all guided trips) walk Rapid 9, known as Commercial Suicide, before sliding into Rapid 10, The Gnashing Jaws of Death, a wave train that's not quite as scary as its name implies. Even more massive waves await in Rapid 13, The Mother; some have said the plunge from the first wave (which is actually the convergence of two waves) is enough to make your stomach drop. The Zambezi's most famous run is Rapid 18, aptly nicknamed Oblivion. It consists of three waves, with the third being the biggest and best. More than a few paddlers have injected a little excitement into an uninspired workday by YouTubing a bit of Oblivion carnage.

A great majority of the over thirty thousand visitors who run the Zambezi each year will take out at Rapid 23, Morning Shave, and climb—perhaps a bit tired and sunburned—the 750 feet from the take-out and toast their successful run with a cold beer or soda. Another option, one enjoyed by fewer than five hundred people a year, is to continue downriver. "If you opt to head downstream, you leave all the commercial outfits behind," John said. "There are beautiful white beaches for camping. You're not likely to see any of the animal life that people might hope to see on a safari—the gradient is too fast for crocodiles and hippos, and the gorge too steep for other animals to negotiate. But the people are gone, and you're left with just the sound of the water." Though the Zambezi tames considerably as you descend below the one-day float take-out, several more rapids await, including Upper Moemba, which is larger than any of the previous runs you'll have encountered.

JOHN BERRY has African roots dating back to 1820. He grew up in KwaZulu-Natal. After a first life in South Africa's corporate world as an engineer, John exchanged collar and tie for shorts and rafters when he formed Zambezi Safari & Travel. Today, he serves as the company's managing director from his office in the United Kingdom. John serves on the board of the African Travel and Tourism Association. When not in the U.K. office, he can be found on a mountain bike with mates, walking or swimming with the family Labradors, or traveling.

If You Go

▶ **Getting There:** Most visitors fly to Livingstone, Zambia, via Johannesburg. Service is available via British Airways (800-247-9297; www.ba.com) and South African Airways (+27 11 978 1234; www.flysaa.com).

▶ **Best Time to Visit:** One-day trips are run year-round (with the possible exception of March and April), though the river is most exciting August through February; multiday trips are offered from August through mid-November.

▶ **Guides/Outfitters:** A number of companies lead day and multiday trips on the Zambezi, including Zambezi Rafting (303-988-5037; www.zambezirafting.com).

▶ **Level of Difficulty:** Though there are many Class V rapids, visitors taking a guided trip do not need previous paddling experience.

▶ **Accommodations:** The Livingstone Tourism Association (www.livingstonetourism .com) highlights lodging options.

DESTINATION

50

Published in 2014 by Stewart, Tabori & Chang
An imprint of ABRAMS

Text copyright © 2014 Chris Santella

Photograph credits: Page 2: Gary Luhm Photography; Page 8: Photo taken by No Roads Expeditions, noroads
.com.au; Page 12: Justin Bailie/TandemStock.com; Page 14: Frits Meyst/MeystPhoto.com; Page 16: Wendy Doughty,
Kayak Adventures Worldwide; Page 22: Photo Copyright Al Bakker; Page 26: Justin Bailie/Aurora Photos; Page
30: Andrew Bain; Page 34: Michael Hanson/Aurora Photos; Page 38: Photo by Zachary Collier/Northwest Rafting
Company; Page 42: Spirit of the West Adventures (www.kayakingtours.com); Page 46: Bruce Kirby, Nahanni.com;
Page 50: Stephen Welch - ARTA River Trips; Page 56: Altue Seakayaking; Page 60: David Boswell/DBoswell
Photography; Page 64: Courtesy of Austin Adventures; Page 68: Tom Till, O.A.R.S.; Page 72: Carol Barrington/
Aurora Photos; Page 78: Sea kayak guide/Stelios Asmargianakis; Page 80: Rod Feldtmann; Page 84: Na Pali
Kayak; Page 92: © Haukursig.com; Page 96: Justin Bailie/TandemStock.com; Page 102: Leon Werdinger
Photography; Page 108: © Tommaso Di Girolamo/FirstLight.com; Page 112: Luke Wettstein, Adventure-Cambodia;
Page 120: Kenneth Winiarski & Dave ConleyPage 124: Michelle Bowman; Page 130: Gary Luhm Photography; Page
132: Brian O'Keefe; Page 136: Glacier Raft Company; Page 140: Rob Suisted/www.naturespic.com; Page 144: Terry
Parker, Nahanni.com; Page 150: © Gary and Joanie McGuffin; Page 154: Colin Moneypenny; Page 160: Justin
Bailie/TandemStock.com; Page 162: Justin Bailie/TandemStock.com; Page 166: Louise Southerden; Page 172:
Davide Scagliola/Parallelozero/Aurora Photos; Page 174: Photo by Boreal River guide, Danny Peled; Page 178:
Photo by Zachary Collier/Northwest Rafting Company; Page 182: Angus Nicol; Page 186: Drew Gregory; Page 192:
Frits Meyst/MeystPhoto.Com; Page 198: Rick Sweitzer; Page 204: xPACIFICA/Aurora Photos; Page 208: Photo:
Reid Morth; Page 216: Harrison Shull/Aurora Photos; Page 220: Chad Ehlers/Aurora Photos

Library of Congress Control Number: 2014930930

ISBN: 978-1-61769-125-6

Editor: Samantha Weiner
Designer: Anna Christian
Production Manager: Kathleen Gaffney
Fifty Places series design by Paul G. Wagner

This book was composed in Interstate, Scala, and Village.

Printed and bound in China
10 9 8 7 6 5 4 3 2 1

Stewart, Tabori & Chang books are available at special discounts when purchased in quantity for premiums
and promotions as well as fundraising or educational use. Special editions can also be created to specification.
For details, contact specialsales@abramsbooks.com or the address below.

ABRAMS
THE ART OF BOOKS SINCE 1949

115 West 18th Street
New York, NY 10011
www.abramsbooks.com